Psalms

FOR THE
SINGLE MOM

LISA HUSSEY

Karla:
merry Christmas!
I hope you are doing
Well. I think & pray
for you all often.
Love Jana
Meagan & John
'99

Psalms
FOR THE
SINGLE MOM

LISA HUSSEY

Chariot Victor Publishing
A Division of Cook Communications

Chariot Victor Publishing,
Cook Communications, Colorado Springs, Colorado 80918
Cook Communications, Paris, Ontario
Kingsway Ccommunications, Eastbourne, England

PSALMS FOR THE SINGLE MOM
© 1999 by Lisa Hussey.
Printed in the United States of America.

Editor: Wendy Peterson
Design: Big Cat Marketing Communications

1 2 3 4 5 6 7 8 9 10 Printing/Year 03 02 01 00 99

All Scripture quotations are taken from the *New American Standard Bible*®, Copyright © 1960, 1962, 1963, 1968, 1971, 1972, 1973, 1975, 1977, 1995 by the Lockman Foundation. Used by permission.

CIP Coming

Dedication

This book is dedicated to

The Reverend Wayne L. Williams
of
Marietta, Georgia.

He took my shattered soul and gently pieced me back together.

By listening, telling fables, making me face up to the truth, he helped me learn to love myself.

So Wayne,
minister, teacher extraordinaire, poet,
avid cyclist, player of bongos, and
fellow right brainer,

this one's
for you.

Contents

Introduction

This is a book of heart songs. It is a pouring out, a slice of soul offered on a plate of experiences. It resonates with real feelings as varied and intricate as life itself. It is the story of one woman's journey through single motherhood.

Each of us, at some moment, is there. We stand alone, making life's decisions for these children we live with and love. At times we resent the responsibility; we feel as if our very veins have been tapped and the blood that is our strength is seeping out of us and into these hungry, all-consuming beings. Other times, we hold out what we have to offer on the palms of our hands and watch with wonder as it is picked up and gently woven into the little lives that share ours. We may be single because of death or divorce or because our husbands are away either physically, emotionally, or both. In every case, we each experience the depth and breadth of isolation that the tight grip of single motherhood has on our hearts, on our innermost beings, on who we are and who we become. But from that isolation can come new strength, new insight, increased knowledge of all we are capable of accomplishing. We can become bulwarks for our children, protecting them as we guide, urge, and nurture them; strong walls held together with the mortar of hope. Some days, parts of us crumble either privately or right out there for all the world to see. Other days, we add thickness and detail—new assurances that we do have it together after all.

I invite you on this journey with me. What follows are frozen moments remembered—pearls from a string of time. It is my hope that you will find some of yourself here, that you will realize the range and intensity of emotions you undergo and have indeed felt before. The most enriching, satisfying experience in the world—that of being a mother—can at times be the most demanding, deflating, and demoralizing, especially when it is attempted alone. The relentlessness of both life and children can be overwhelming.

So lift your heart with mine, and let it sing. Let it moan and cry and gnash its very teeth. The depth to which it grieves is the height to which it can celebrate! Let it experience the very realness of the old adage that sorrow is a clever miner: the deeper it mines into your heart, the more joy you can contain.

A Promise Kept

Blessed be the God and Father of our Lord
Jesus Christ, the Father of mercies and God
of all comfort, who comforts us in all our
affliction so that we will be able to comfort
those who are in any affliction with the
comfort with which we ourselves are
comforted by God. (2 Cor. 1:3-4)

This is the story
        of a journey I embarked on
        with God and with my three sons:
                Sean, Neil, and Jeff.
It started eight years ago
        and was at first filled with equal
                amounts of pain and triumph.
As I grew in faith, wisdom, experience, and
                strength,
        the moments of victory increased
        and began to outweigh the troubled
                times.

I wished often
        that I had someone to inspire me, to
                lead me,
        to whisper, "You can make it"—
        "Jesus with skin on," my dear friend
                Judy May would say.
I needed people to help me along the way—

1

people with shoulders to cry on,
hands to lift me up when I'd fallen,
feet to deliver a kick in the rear when
    self-pity settled in.

As God provided those people,
    I promised Him that I would take all
        the pain
        I've been experiencing
    and use it to encourage others who are
        at various points on this journey
        of single motherhood—
those who may be tempted to give in,
  letting bitterness enter their hearts.
This book of heart songs,
        soul searches,
        mind stretches,
        and, hopefully, humor
is the fulfillment of that promise.

If it touches just one single mom;
if it makes her load a little lighter,
    her guilt that she's not perfect a little
        less;
if it allows her to gently laugh at herself;
if it gives her the strength to keep loving
  herself and her children,
    to not give up on taking care of her own
        needs as well as those of her
        children
    (for you can only give what you have, I
        have discovered,

and if you're on empty in the self-
   esteem department,
you won't have much with which to
   saturate your children);
then it will have served its purpose.

God has blessed me with the opportunity to
   begin anew.
He has given me three fine sons to raise.
He has used my parents,
Bill and Rhoda Hussey, to support me,
   inspire me, challenge me, and be the
      undergirding to the belief that
      I could do all things through Christ
      who strengthens me.
He had, in His wisdom, had them raise me
   in a way that instilled in me
      such a fierce sense of independence,
         such a stubbornness,
      that I refused to give up, to give in, or
         to run home.

What follows flowed from my heart.
I pray it touches yours.

That Word—Divorce

My fingers trembled, I remember.
My throat went dry.
The words were trapped,
    stuck in my windpipe
    by choking sobs of helplessness
        and rage.

"I need to talk to you about
    f-f-filing for
    d-d-d-divorce."

Finally, the word squeezed past my taut lips
    and fell into the telephone receiver,
    then into the attorney's ear.

Divorce? Unspeakable!

Hadn't I been trying to avoid this very word
    for more than five years?
Christians don't get divorced, I firmly
        believed,
    as I prayed, pleaded,
    compromised, and rationalized
    my way through the months
        that piled into years.

When you're caught in a downward spiral
    directed by someone else's irresponsibility,
    it's near impossible
        to fight your way back up alone.

4

It's like one of those dreams
    where your legs are weighted
    as heavy as if they were cast from iron.
You're struggling to the surface,
    but your heavy legs hold you back,
    not allowing you to break free.

I was drowning
    in a sea of lies, foreclosure,
    verbal abuse, and filth.
It was sink or grab the life raft
    named the S.S. *Divorce,*
    which would take me, I knew full well,
    not into the Sea of Tranquillity
        but into the Bay of Chaos,
        through the Strait of Faith,
        into the Start Again Sea.

Refugee Momma

"We're hungry, Momma!"
Their piteous cries were matched only by
      the starved look in their eyes.
I couldn't stand it anymore.
I picked up the phone;
I watched myself dialing Pizza Hut.
"Send out a large pepperoni," I crowed.
They cheered—stunned, disbelieving.
"Isn't it too much money?" one asked me.
"Not tonight!" I answered.

I rationalized it by telling myself there were
      no groceries in the pantry.
The boys and I were moving out next week,
     right after our court date for
        preliminary custody.
My soon-to-be ex-husband had been
      consuming whatever food I brought in
    while we were at school and day care.
He was not here tonight;
    that was cause enough for celebration.

I reached for our joint checkbook.
One more time I'd pray the check didn't
      bounce.
Tonight I prayed halfheartedly; I didn't care.
My boys would eat pizza—regardless.

It arrived in a cloud of spices and tangy
      steam.
Tomato and pepperoni smells wrapped
      themselves around four sets of
      nostrils
    and drew them toward the thin brown
      box.
The door closed behind the pizza man, and
      I shouted,
    "Upstairs! To the bonus room!"

I remember opening the box.
I remember the image—frozen in my mind
      forever—
    of three little wolf cubs, ages two, four,
      and six,
    poised over their captured prey, tongues
      between lips, ready to pounce.
I don't recall if we had napkins, plates, or
      drinks.
I do recall how starved I was.
But one look at their faces, and I drew back,
      saying,
    "Help yourselves, boys!"

Cheese strung between box and slice,
Sauce seeped down chins.
Smiles lit up the three tiny faces,
    the haunted, hungry look chased away
      by glorious pizza.

They ate until there was nothing left but the
      backs—

the crescent spines of hard crust.
They sat back—satiated, replete.
"Thanks, Momma! Thanks, Momma!" they
      echoed.
    Then they lay against the couch cushions,
    each a satisfied heap of tousled blond
      hair and bulging tummy,
    lost in Looney Tunes.
I closed the box and took it downstairs.
It was not until I reached the kitchen
    that I lifted the lid and grabbed one
      hard crescent for me.
It was my only actual bite of that pizza.
The boys never knew.

But that image of the three of them
    falling upon that pepperoni pizza
    fed my soul
    just as it ripped it apart.

It shouldn't be like this.
It doesn't *have* to be like this.

I was a refugee momma, feeding my starving
    sons,
    and we were about to break *free*.

It Makes People Uncomfortable, Lord

"We're getting a divorce, we're buying a
      barn, but we're not remarried yet."

The words fluttered out of Sean's six-year-
      old mouth, blue eyes flashing,
        as he looked way up at the tall elderly
        woman
      in the checkout line at Kroger.
She smiled sympathetically, first at him, and
      then at me.
Shortly, thereafter,
                she switched lanes.

It makes people uncomfortable, Lord.
I know, because it makes me nervous
      as *heck*.
Two weeks we've been on our own.
I look down at my sweet bundle of boys:
      Sean, an eager, wiggly six year old;
      Neil, a four-year-old ball of perpetual
        motion;
      and Jeff, a bumbly blond bear, just two,
        still a baby.

How are we going to make it, Lord?
How can I be everything I need to be for
      these three
      and still take care of myself?

How am I going to get up at 5:30 each
            morning;
      get three boys ready, fed;
      pack lunches, book bags, diaper bags;
      and get out the door
      with some semblance of sanity
      when I'm not even a morning person?

Two weeks into this thing and my ex-husband's
            words haunt me already:
      "You're never going to be able to make
            it on your own!
      You're stuck with these three boys, and
            you'll be worn slap out.
      Nobody's ever going to want you again . . ."

I look around me, at the early-sixties,
            gold/green/orange interior
of this barn-shaped house I'm renting.
I see my face fragmented in the twenty-four
            mirrored tiles on the kitchen wall.

"I want me," I say to my myriad of reflections.
"And that
            is enough."

ALONE AGAIN

I wanted someone to hold me.
I hungered for arms wrapped around me,
                    snug,
                    warm,
                    tight.

I lay there
        shivering
            in my scratchy-stiff sheets.

And thought I'd die
    if someone didn't hold me soon.

Rub my back,
Curl his legs around mine,
Fit me into him, back to front, like spoons.

"Hold me,
        just hold me,"
                I went whispering into the
                night.

Suddenly, jangles and light
    announced morning.
I shook myself awake
    and realized I was alone
                again.

SINGLE NAME ON A DOUBLE SPORTS ROSTER

If I could write a country song, I'd call it:
  "Single Name on a Double Sports
      Roster."

Because that's me
    every time one of my children
    is on another baseball/soccer/
        basketball/tennis/*any* sport team.

When they pass out the team roster,
it says,
    Tom and Betty
    Bob and Cathy
    Jim and Debbie
and then
    Lisa
then back to
    Randy and Cindy
    Phil and Nancy
and so on.

My eyes burn, and I get a walnut in my throat
    when I see my name

            isolated

    on that page.

It sits there

            alone,

12

some sort of proof that I am not connected,
   that I'm doing this solo.

It's so black-and-white.
So concrete.

Somehow it shouts failure
  as it whispers
    hide,
    don't expose yourself,
    protect.

I fold up the roster
  and carry it with a heavy heart to my car.
I plunk down on the driver's seat
and wallow in self-pity.

Minutes pass
  before a still, small voice
    breathes to my soul.

I fumble in my purse for a pencil
and amend the roster,
adding a "God and"
  before the Lisa.

> "And lo, I am with
> you always, even to
> the end of the age."
>   (Matt. 28:20)

13

QUITTER

I won't be a quitter, Lord!
You made me stronger than that.
I won't quit; I don't care HOW hard it gets!
I grit my teeth and say it most loudly
    on the days I mean it the least.

No, You say.
It's okay to quit.

Whatever could You mean, Lord?

And then I see.

Sometimes it takes more strength, more
        guts, to quit.

Quit worrying, You whisper; trust Me.
Quit holding grudges; forgive.
Quit procrastinating; do it now.
Quit being afraid; accept My Spirit of
        confidence.
Quit hating yourself; forgive, accept,
        and love.
Quit trying to do it all yourself; accept
        My help.
Quit criticizing others; work on changing
        yourself.
Quit doubting; believe!

Okay, Lord,

I'll be a quitter for You.
I have a feeling
    that's the only way
I'll ever truly win.

WHO AM I?

Who *am* I?
Now that I'm no longer married,
    am I Lisa Hussey again?
    Or am I still Lisa Dearman?
I've been Lisa Hussey longer, but Lisa
        Dearman more recently.
My sons' last name is Dearman.
    Do I want to have a different last name
        than they have?
Does it matter?
    "What's in a name?" Shakespeare asked
        long ago.
A lot, I'd say.
    How do I sign my checks?
    What do my students call me at school?
    Am I *Mrs.* Dearman, even though I'm
        not married?
    Does *Ms.* Dearman sound too liberal?
    What name do I write on all my teaching
        things in permanent marker?

I've had lots of students whose moms have
        remarried,
    and then they have still another different
        last name.
It's so confusing, and sometimes I've had
        parents get defensive

if I call them by the child's last name
    instead of their own.
I've known some families who have received
    the principal's permission
        to "let" the children use the new step-
        parent's last name
and then others who have gone ahead and
    adopted the children
        and changed the name legally.
If it's confusing to me, as an adult,
    how much more it must bewilder a
    child.

Who am I?
Maybe I should be Lisa Hussman!

I'm Not After Your Husband

"Hey!" I wanted to shout. "You silly,
        insecure woman!
    I am *not* 'after' your husband!
He was very nice to help me carry my
        ice chest
    full of soft drinks for the soccer team;
but when I smiled and thanked him,
    it was *not* an invitation.
It was one person appreciating another's
        kindness.
That's it."

What is it about being a divorced woman
    that makes the women around her
    wary, suspect, and sometimes downright
        cold?
I just got out of pain, of emotional drain
        with one man.
I'm in no condition to jump in
    right away with another.
And even if I were, I wouldn't choose
        yours—
    he's yours; you keep him.

I just want to be treated as a person,
    with kindness, compassion, sensitivity,
        and dignity.
I will treat you the same way.

18

Please, please include me!
Invite my children and me to dinner, to
        outings, to parties.
We need to see intact families.
We want to be included,
        embraced,
        validated.
Don't isolate us by your own fear and
        insecurity.
We already feel like failures
    in this couples world.
Help us not hide
in humiliated silence,
      but lend us your strength
      to rebuild bridges
      instead of constructing walls.

Reach out a hand
    and pull us into your world.

We'll *both* be richer for it.

Why Me, Lord?

Why me, Lord?
What did I do that was so bad
 that I would end up sleeping diagonally
  across a queen-size bed,
 crying into my pillows after I pummel
  them with fists of rage?
Hot tears of exhaustion fill them instead of
  down;
I swear they'd drip bitterness if I squeezed
  them.

My thoughts zigzag, spiraling wildly up and
  nosediving into my pale, striped
  comforter:
 I can't do it anymore!
 I can't be everything to my sons!
 There are three of them, one of me, and
  they are younger, have more stamina.
 They outlast me!

I'm so sleepy, Lord, and yet I can't sleep.
I can't turn off the worries inside my head.
Where will I get the money to send them to
  college?
Why aren't elementary teachers paid more?
Wait, forget college, where will I get the
  money to pay the light bill,
 to buy three sets of school pictures,

to buy new sneakers for the feet that
    grow too quickly
and seem to make a hobby out of
    dragging toes on sidewalks and
    through puddles?

Oh, Lord, where is that sleep?
Five-thirty comes mighty early, and I need
    some rest.
Rest . . . ?
    I seem to remember,
        "In repentance and rest you will be
        saved,
        In quietness and trust is your
        strength."

                        (Isa. 30:15)

Oh, Lord, remind me of that the next time
    I feel like Charlie Brown in that
        cardboard box,
        saying, "Why me, Lord?"
    When I get so overwhelmed I feel like
        I'm racing around a hamster's wheel,
        and I fall asleep tutoring
                and during sermons
                and in the middle of
                teachers' meetings.

Quietness and trust
and resting
    in You.

New Beginnings

When a crystal vase slips from fingers
     and shatters on a marble floor;
when an egg is smashed,
     its ragged shell fragments scattered;
when the petals of a rose are torn off and
       bruised,
     crushed beneath the wind's weight—
there is no fixing it.

Not so with human lives.
We can go on.
With us
    there are new beginnings,
    a crisp white sheet of paper
       on which to write the words of today.

Trusting Again

How do I take the first step toward trusting
again, Lord?
How do I loosen the grip that fear-driven
survival has on my heart?
I want to believe,
but someone has let me down so badly,
so often,
and has filled my life with so many lies
that I hardly know the truth anymore.

Some things were said about me, Lord.
Horrible things. Lies.
My character was even maligned to my sons.
Anger does weird things to people. So does
hurt.
Be careful of rage, I want to warn those I
care for.
Be careful of the hatred that is the cancer of
the soul.
Its by-product is the ooze of bitterness that
fills every inner recess of your heart.

Tears help. So does talking. But as a wise
man once told me,
you have to use discretionary disclosure.
You have to be careful to whom you
tell what.

You must put strong walls around your
          hurting heart
     and not allow those who would judge
          you near your innermost being;
     those who have never walked your
          footsteps,
     have never felt the degree of pain you
          have felt.
You must not give away all of your golden
          treasure.
Reserve some; you never know what lies
          ahead,
     and you just may need some sooner
          than you think.
Walks help too. Long walks filled with soul-
          searching as well as mindlessness.
Empty-headed ditties sung to the babble of
          brooks
     under bridges leading nowhere.

How did we take the first step, Lord, You
          and I?
     That tiny step toward letting go;
     giving up bitterness before it solidified
          into resentment?
It was oh-so-small, really.
     Just a little beginning,
     a gleam of forgiveness that led into
     the shine of peace.
It was putting one shaking foot at the edge
          of the cliff
     and stepping off . . .

HIKING

My friends tease me on the weekends that
 I have the boys,
 when they can't get hold of me and
 have to leave phone messages.
They call me "Super Mom" and laughingly
 say that I'm probably out there
 hiking or something again.
They are probably right.

I can't think of a better place to take three
 restless boys who love to explore!
What else would I do—drag them to the
 mall?
 "Here, boys, here are the fancy, designer
 clothes you won't be wearing . . ."
 "Look, but can't have . . ."
 "We'll try on the next batch of hand-
 me-downs or trek over to the local
 discount store."
 No sir! Not my boys!

When we get new clothes,
 it's with excitement,
 it's what we can afford,
 and it's special and fun and uplifting.
I don't set them up for disappointment.
I don't take them where they'll see things
 they can't have.

We go to the woods. Kennesaw Mountain.
We climb with backpacks stuffed with
> oranges and raisins,
> > apples and juice boxes.
We have canteens swinging at our sides,
> along with binoculars and jackets tied
> > around our waists.
We sing, we whoop, we run.
We imagine.
Each boy finds the perfect walking stick
> and uses it until it's time to go,
> > leaving it then for someone else.

There's a huge rock that looks like several
> elephants,
> and they love to play safari on that
> and look far off into the distance as they
> > stand on its top.

Sometimes we take friends along,
> and every once in a while we run into
> > someone we know.
> But most times, it's the four of us,
> > hiking vigorously and loving it.
> Time after time after time.

I don't take them there to be "Super Mom."
I hope I allow them the greatest gifts of all:
> receiving life and all you've been given
> > with gratitude,
> discovering all that your body is capable
> > of doing,
> experiencing nature in all its glory,

and reveling in the sheer irreplaceable
value of fun.
Fun for fun's sake.
Lost, I think, too easily at the mall.

ARUBA

"Oh, you simply *must* go to Aruba, Lisa!
It is *fabulous*!"

The words stung,
> mainly for their obliviousness to my
> > situation
> rather than any cruel intent,
> for their lack of sensitivity
> and shortness of empathy.

There really is something to this
> "walk a mile in someone else's
> > moccasins" stuff.
"Let me show you my latest photos of the
> > Caribbean"
> doesn't cut it when there's no money—
> > even for a trip to Dairy Queen.

Don't rub it in, I want to whisper.
Don't be such a contrast
> that I'm tempted to feel sorry for myself.
Please take your beautiful four-by-six glossies
> and leave me to my summer reruns
> and my Diet Coke with lemon squeezed
> > in it
> > for that taste of the islands.

No White Knights
on the Horizon

I told people I was *not* waiting for my
        white knight to come "fix" my life.
And I meant it!

Until I met a guy who swept me off my feet—
And then I believed he was the
        answer to all my problems.

But he was so strict with my kids.
Well, wasn't that what they needed?
        A firm male influence?
        Someone to guide them?
        Strength?
But a tiny voice deep inside me questioned,
        was it *really* necessary to send them
          upstairs to their rooms
        because they wouldn't eat the Brussels
          sprouts
        he had brought over?
Dear Gussie, *I* didn't even like the wretched
        things!

He was so *sure* of everything.
"No Cokes at Taco Bell! We'll all drink
        water." (We will?)
"A deposit at the video store? Forget it—
        we don't want the movie after all
        that we've just spent forty-five
        minutes selecting.

And quit your whining, kids!"

It didn't take long before his armor lost its
      silvery gleam.
Lawyer, looks and all, he didn't wear well.
He *created* problems where there hadn't
      been any before.
He was arrogant, opinionated, and controlling.

As he exited from my life, a great truth
      entered:
    No one can fix your life.
    There are *no* white knights.
I had to be prepared to do this all on my
      own, with God's help, for always.
There may *never* be anyone to help me raise
      my children.
But "I can do all things through Him who
      strengthens me."
And I can certainly do it without opinionated,
      Brussels sprouts-toting
white knights!

REGRETS

Regrets are weird things.

They come into my heart with soft-padded
      cat's feet,
    silently wrapping steel-sharp wire
      around the outside of it;
    then pulling—hard!—
    ripping the very core of me.

The pieces land soggy:
    three-day-old cornflakes
    piling in the pit of my stomach,
    curdling, souring.

A song stirs a memory,
    and I begin to think of all
      the could-have-beens,
    the what-ifs,
    the why-nots.

Stop! I tell myself.
You can't do this to yourself.
You are where you are.

Deal with it.

This I recall to my mind,
Therefore I have hope.
The Lord's lovingkindnesses indeed never
      cease,

For His compassions never fail.
They are new every morning;
Great is Your faithfulness.
"The Lord is my portion," says my soul,
"Therefore I have hope in Him."

(Lam. 3:21-24)

Begin a new morning, I tell myself.
Go the only direction you can—forward—
making the Lord your portion
and living in great faithfulness and soaring
hope.

Those two have a way of crowding out
regrets.

BLIND DATE

How in the world did I get talked into
       this, Lord?
    A blind date?
    At my age?
A rivulet of sweat is running from the small
       of my back down my legs.
My mouth has turned to cotton.

What will we talk about?
What if he's a real jerk?
What if he's too goofy for words?
What is the minimum number of minutes
       you're required
    to stay on a blind date?
Why won't my hair do anything I want
       it to?
What if he thinks I look old?
What if he freaks when he finds out I have
       children?

Okay, I tell the reflection in the mirror,
I can do this.
Hey, he's a friend of Sue's, right?
He couldn't be *that* bad.

Well, come to think of it, he's really some-
       one Sue's husband works with.
Did she say if she'd actually ever *met* him?

Oh, dear, the sitter's here.
Where's my other shoe?
Did I ever put blush on? Oh, no, now I put
      on too much.
   "Hello, I'm Shirley Temple," I can say as
      I open the door.
Am I truly singing "I Have Confidence"
      from *The Sound of Music*?
I've lost it—call the men in the white coats.

Confidence.
Come on, Lisa, confidence.
Just be yourself.
Take a deep breath.
And go downstairs . . .

ENVIRONMENTALLY
SENSITIVE

Someone once told me that I am extremely
environmentally sensitive.
I think this meant that, rather than my
getting my feelings hurt
about ecology,
my surroundings play a big part in how I feel.
I never knew how true this was
until the year I hated everywhere I had
to be.

I'd already decided that I hated the interior
of the house I was renting:
the colors, the carpet, the lack of light,
the dark paneling.
But going to school in the soft gray tones of
the interior of my car
to spend the day surrounded by the
bright colors
of the atmosphere I'd created in my
own brand-new classroom,
with its gorgeous carpet and cabinets,
made the evening hours more palatable.

Then two things happened that changed
all that.
First, I was moved out of the school building
to a "portable classroom" (a trailer)

standing on the back field of the
    school yard.
The inside was dirty, old, plain, blah.
It seemed to rain almost every day,
and I lost count of how many of my
    shoes got ruined.
Second, my car was having continual
    problems,
ranging from small to major,
and my loving, wonderful dad got me
    another car
and drove it down from Kansas City.
I was thrilled and touched beyond words,
and I don't want to seem ungrateful,
but the interior of the car is red—I
    mean RED—
and it really gets to me, not just after
    awhile,
    but immediately!

Now no matter where I am that's "mine,"
    I hate it.
Something irritates me constantly in the
    places I live and work—
    the spaces where I am supposed to
    accomplish great things
    or go to relax or to *get to* the relaxing
    spots!
Where is the break, the solace, the respite
    from eye agony?
That's the year I decided to forget it all
    and go home to Kansas City.

I'd lay awake in bed at night,
    designing a cozy, charming cottage the
        boys and I would live in.
I'd think up my ideal classroom.
I'd drool over cars with neutral interiors.

If only my circumstances would change,
    I'd be so much happier.
Slowly, a bitterness I had not experienced
        before
    crept in,
along with a realization that running away
        never solves anything.
It postpones it, but it doesn't get to the
        heart of the issue—
    which is acceptance.
If only, if only . . .
I would have to find peace in Atlanta before
        going anywhere else;
    peace in a dark, dreary house, a dirty
        old trailer, and red car seats.

You taught me, Lord, that You are bigger
        than circumstances.
In *all* things, give praise.
Not just when my environmental
        sensitivities are soothed,
but even when—most especially when—
        they're not.

Shake That Dust off Your Feet

"Whoever does not receive you, nor
   heed your words, as you go out of
   that house or that city, shake the
   dust off your feet." (Matt. 10:14)

It happened again today, Lord, another
      reference to "those single mothers."
As if, just by virtue of being single, you're
      naturally careless
                              or wanton
                              or immoral.
You leave your children untended for hours.
You spend their child support on fake
      fingernails.
You ignore their schoolwork.

Someone was relating an account of a
      terrible fire
   in which the entire house burned down.
In the telling, they let it be known that it
      was a single mom
   who had been having a birthday party
      for her child,
   and a coal from the barbecue grill had
      fallen beneath the deck.
I watched as others listened, nodding their
      heads.
Was the general consensus that single moms

are inattentive,
poor grill watchers, or just unable to
detect a spark or put out a fire?

Certainly, as a teacher, I've heard it stated
very matter-of-factly
that a certain child is from a *single-
parent family*—
more politically correct than the former
phrase *broken home*—
and that one could attribute many of
the child's problems
to that one fact alone.

No one knows, until they have walked in
your shoes, day after day.
The sheer, hard, thankless job many single
mothers do that goes unnoticed,
until they slip up.
The grueling pace that never lets up.
The details you can get lost in.
The weight of responsibility that can crush you.

I have decided, Lord, that,
along with others not hearing or
responding to Your Gospel,
if people cannot receive us for who we are,
we are to shake the dust off our feet and
go on
and not waste any precious time
worrying about the opinions of
people who unfairly misjudge us.
We don't owe anyone but You an explanation.
Period. Amen.

Tape on the Bottom of My Shoe

Lord, I want to thank You today especially
        for my friend Pam Dean.
She can make me laugh faster and harder
        than anyone I know!
I *need* people in my life who can help me
        laugh at myself
    when I tend to take life, and me, a little
        too seriously,
    and when I'm dealing with as many
        weighty issues as I am.
Thank You for the crazy cards she sends by
        way of her students
    to my classroom.
Her hilarious teaching stories.
Her quick wit.

I remember one day, I had completely fallen
        apart
    about something.
And she said, "Lisa! This is *not* a big deal!
    This is tape stuck to the bottom of
        your shoe!
    It's irritating and you want it to go away,
    but it's *not* life-threatening.
    Save it for the really big stuff.
    Now relax, deal with it,
    and get used to the 'twok' sound of the
        tape!"

40

I remind myself of that quite often.

Amazing how You can use people to teach
me such profound things, Lord!
And how wonderful that You choose to do
it through humor!

KEEP YOUR EYES INSIDE THE CAR

It was twilight on a Friday night,
  and the four of us zoomed through the
    plush subdivision
  on a mission to deliver Sean to the
    home of his friend Mark
  to spend the night.

"We're late," groaned Sean.
"We're always late!" I laughed. "Lisa is my
    middle name.
  My first name is Last-Minute!"
We all laughed. It was an old joke.
"Which street, Sean?" I asked.
I always get so mixed up in Walker's Ridge,
  so many streets veering off from one
    another,
  making circles and cul-de-sacs.
"Take a left. And then your next right.
    Fourth house down."
I smiled. No wonder I called Sean my
  walking map.

We raced up to Mark's house, and Mark
    burst out the front door.
"Hey man, Where *were* you?"
  and then as an afterthought, "Oh, hey,
    Mrs. Dearman."
"Bye, Swe—," the door slammed on my

word as Sean,
backpack slung over his shoulder,
made his way laughing to Mark's house
and waved back to me.
"Okay, guys. Next stop, Blockbuster Video,"
I sang.

As we threaded our way back out of the
neighborhood,
a quiet hung over the car.
I drove slower, and the evening hush
rested around the beautiful houses.
I glanced to the left and saw a gorgeous,
elegant dining room, softly lit.
Silk flowers on the table.
Rich floral wallpaper gracing the walls.
So beautiful.
One house floated by after the other.
Their glorious window treatments were
certainly made for looks
rather than privacy,
and it was easy to see into many of the
front rooms.

Suddenly, my heart was wrenched with the
most awful pain.
Why do *they* get this, and I don't?
Lord, it doesn't seem fair.
What did I do that was so wrong that I
keep getting punished for it?
Self-pity dripped over my head, stinging my
eyes.
My shoulders drooped with the hundred-

pound weights of *why* and *me*.
The fun of the evening slowly sank, covered
    over with the sludge of sadness.
I wallowed in it, rolled around, covering
    myself like a pig in mud.
And, of course, my boys pulled in some of
    its essence too.

We were a glum group by the time we got
    home
    with our semiwarm pizza
    and our Disney movie, *Apple Dumpling
    Gang*—
    "for the forty thousandth time," I
    inwardly grumbled.
And I had done it.
Poor me. I didn't get what I wanted.
    No gorgeous house.
    No custom window treatments.
Mine were bargain plastic miniblinds.
I got gypped.

"Help me, Lord," I prayed,
"even on rotten nights like tonight
to be thankful for what I have,
too numerous to list, but certainly headed by
    three healthy sons,
    a loving family in Kansas City,
    an excellent job in a profession I dearly
    love,
    and my own health."

"Next time," You seemed to whisper, "keep
    your eyes inside the car, Lisa."

SINKING IN CHOCOLATE

Pass the malted milk balls, please.

I'm low.

I mean *down*—

> so down I don't care about
> thighs that rub together
> and jeans that are too tight
> and size 8s.

Get off my TV Cindy Crawford!
I want someone real.
I want to laugh through my tears.
Give me someone *real*.
I'm feeling it tonight . . .

> the loneliness,
> the failure,
> the not fitting in,
> the singleness,
> all the decisions, alone,
> all the responsibility, alone,
> all the unfairness of it all.

I can't *stand* it sometimes.

And I want to shout, "I HATE THIS!"
    right in the middle of Sunday School.

So pass me that big ol' milk carton of

malted milk balls.

And let me, just for tonight,
                drown my sorrow
                        in chocolate.

THE REWARD

We turned the corner quickly,
   racing on our way to an errand,
when we saw it.

A black leather wallet
   in the middle of the street—
   ripe for the picking.
We got there first.

I slowed down and scooped it up.
"Oh, no!" I said. "This is full of credit cards!
Someone's really going to be distressed!"
I turned the car back and headed for home.

The doorbell rang.
A tall, thin man, nervously twisting his
         baseball cap in his hands,
      stood on my front porch.
Behind him were a woman and a small girl.
"You called and said you found my wallet,"
         he said.
"Come in—please—it's so cold out there," I
         smiled as I stretched
      his wallet out to him.

"You don't know . . . you have no idea . . ."
         he sputtered.
"I had so many credit cards.

I was afraid some young punk would find it
    and go on a spending spree.
I must've left it on top of my car
    after I was working on the engine . . ."

"You are so kind," his wife said.
My boys turned their gazes toward me and
       beamed.

"Here, take this," the man said, withdrawing
      a twenty dollar bill
    from his newly recovered wallet.

"No," I smiled as I pushed it gently away.
"No, it was my pleasure to return your wallet.
    You take that money and take your
      family out to dinner with it."

The family left,
    laughing and shaking their heads in
      disbelief,
    after we had talked a little while longer
      about his love for cars,
      about soccer,
      and about places in New Jersey.

It had impressed my boys
    that I had not taken the reward
    for returning the wallet.
"That was cool, Mom!"

I hadn't really thought of doing anything else.
It just wouldn't have seemed right.
Why should I take something

for doing the right thing?
For doing what God expected me to do?

A month went past.
We saw the wallet family
    at the soccer fields
    and in the neighborhood.
We'd wave and stop to talk.

One day my brake light came on.
I had noticed a weird "feel" to my brakes.
I called my wallet friend
    to ask his opinion
    on the most reputable place
    to get new brakes.

"My house," he surprised me by saying.
"I'll buy the parts and do it for you.
    You can just pay me back for the parts."

Imagine how amazed I was to write him a
        check for $27.17!

You do reap what you sow.
The good comes back.

NEW REALITIES

I've learned to take care of myself—
    to protect my vulnerable emotions,
    to erect boundaries around my boys
        and me
    that say, "Hands off!" and, "Treat with
        respect."
    I guess that's why I haven't gone to
        Easter Sunday service since being
alone.

I've learned not to put myself in places
    where self-pity can etch into what
        progress I'm making,
    where awkwardness can erode my
        newfound self-esteem.

Places like soccer banquets,
        where name cards proclaim
    all the Mr. and Mrs. pairs,
    like sets of salt and pepper shakers.

Church pictorial directory waiting areas,
    trying valiantly to keep three little boys'
        shirttails in,
    their hair plastered down,
    and my spirits up amongst all the
        "regular" families with dads.

And Easter Sundays,

where families are highly visible.
Boys with tiny new sports coats
    are pulled along by high-heeled mothers,
while satin-streamed, lacy girls
    scamper beside their dads.
Each family looks like a Kodak ad,
    swooshing past in perfumed clouds,
    waving madly,
    smiling, smiling,
    calling out to Aunt Lindsay, Uncle Bob,
        and the children
    they'll see at Grandma's
    after they stop at the store for the
        forgotten Sprite and cantaloupe.

I avoid it all.
We make new traditions
    of Easter omelets,
    three backyard egg hunts,
    and retelling the Easter story
    as we huddle, four snuggly bunnies in
        our hutch.

We face our reality in our own way.

As we protect ourselves from too much
        fantasy.

CUTTING A RUG

It was the ugliest color I had ever seen.
And it was the first thing I noticed about
   the house.
Matted down, stained, past worn-out,
   grungy, goldish-brown.
"I can't live with that awful carpet!" I moaned.
But, somehow, for two and a half years now,
   I had managed to alternately ignore and
   tolerate it.

It was one of those things I daily prayed to
   have the strength to accept,
   and yet resented having to.

I learned to guide my eyes upward,
   focusing six inches above its mangy
   surface.
Framed prints graced my walls.
Flowers of peach and cream balancing
   among marbles
   gently drew attention away, away from
   the floor.
My living room had pieces of furniture from
   my pretty house,
   the one with the cream carpet and
   much strife,
   the one I'd left to start over and find
   peace.

They were the colors I adore—
  the rich roses, the soft peach, cream,
   and slate blue.
Overstuffed love seat splattered with
   arrangements of flowers.
A writing desk with elegant Queen Anne legs.
Crystal and porcelain pieces, a brass
   carriage clock.
The mood was airy, fresh, feminine.
It killed me to set it atop that muck.

It was the first room I saw when I came
   bouncing down the stairs
  in the morning;
the last one I viewed before snapping off the
   light
  to wearily creep up them again for bed.
So, when my mom and dad sold my
   original Barbie dolls for me,
I took the money and bought a beautiful
   area rug:
  navy with rose and cream,
  soft, rich-feeling, thick.
It covered the mangy muck
  with only inches of ugliness
   peeking around the edges.
It made *such* a difference, the boys and I
  couldn't believe it.

We all four kept going in to stand at its
   perimeter and gaze at it
  in awe, in wonder.

At first, out of some sort of respect, no one
    would even step on it.
Then, I'm not sure how it started or who
    came up with the idea first,
      we decided to push back the coffee
      table, put on some music,
      and dance.
And boy, DID we dance!
The music was as varied as we were.
So were the moves.
Some moon-walked, some swam,
    or watusied, twisted, jerked, or mash-
    potatoed.
Others free-formed it, making it up as they
    went along.

For hours at a time
    we'd dance!
Dance until our faces glowed,
    until we craved ice water by the
    pitcherful,
    until we dropped heavily onto chairs,
    laughing, satiated,
      eyes glowing, hearts pounding.
We felt so *alive*, so vital,
    so together and united and good.

Once, the boys came up with the idea
    of me being the "Strobe Woman."
Handing me two flashlights, they said,
    "Wave them back and forth like strobes,
    Mom!

No, faster, Mom, *faster!*"
I think I lasted two songs
    before my arms nearly fell off,
    and I permanently retired from being
        Strobe Woman.

Looking back on it now,
    I wonder how a rug could have sparked
        such fun.
A rug
    that in easier times and with much less
        offensive carpet
    would easily have been taken for
        granted
    or even gone entirely unnoticed.

I doubt any of us will ever forget those
        nights of dancing
    or what they did for our spirits.

They are one of the many things
that *no* amount of money,
    from original Barbies or otherwise,
can buy.

PASTA

Lord, I want to thank You for this
        wonderful thing called pasta.
It's easy.
It's cheap.
Boys love it.
And best of all, I can change the shape,
    and they think they're getting
        something new!

Bow ties tonight, boys.
Last night it was seashells.
Tomorrow might be corkscrews.
There's even the size of the shells or the tubes.
The thickness of the spaghetti.
The kind of sauce.

Throw in a little garlic bread, or stale hot-
        dog buns
    broiled open-faced with butter,
and they think it's a feast!

I know that one day soon they'll catch on
        and grow weary of it.
But hey, for now it works.

And if it ain't broke . . .

THREE CUSHIONS WITH DIVIDERS

Who would ever have thought that I
        could get so giddy over a used sofa
    brought home on a drizzly night from
        another teacher's house?
I was!
Positively ecstatic! Thrilled beyond words!
It meant
    no more sore seats from sitting on our
        two-person, oak church pew
        to watch TV;
    a place to cuddle and read and be
        together;
    coziness, warmth, comfort;
    our first "new" piece of furniture
        since being out on our own.

But mostly it meant
    three cushions and two dividers
    so that three boys were each given their
        own territory
    and the instructions, "No fighting!"

And their mother could just possibly
    get a few moments of "down" time
    to veg, to not think, to zone out
    and grab her quickly fleeting sanity . . .
    before the fun starts all over again!

ALL OF US ARE SINGLE MOMS SOMETIMES

I have a tendency
  to think that everything "wrong" with
    my children
  is because I'm single.

  Anything I'm feeling about motherhood
  is peculiar to single moms.

  That I have it so much worse than other
    moms.

Then I talk to moms.
And I listen.
Especially, I listen.

I have found that *most* moms feel alone at
      least some of the time.
Their husbands, if they have one, are
      unavailable at times, preoccupied,
    disinterested, or uneducated about the
      ways of children.
They'd rather leave "that stuff" to their wives.
A lot of moms are floundering out there.
Not every single minute of every day;
most of us do okay most of the time.
But not always.

There are those moments when being a
      good enough mom
    and making instantaneous judgment

calls are nearly impossible;
    when it takes everything we're made of
        and then some.
Times when the washing machine overflows
        the same day as the toilet,
    and while you're fixing that, someone
        lets the dog out
    and tips over the last of the milk *before*
        breakfast.
When every word out of your child's mouth
        seems to be either
    "Stupid!" or "Moron!"
When your son tells you that he needs a
        costume today—
    five minutes before the bus comes.
When all you have is the crusts to make
        sandwiches for the lunches,
    and you are out of juice boxes.
When your head pounds and your heart
        breaks,
    because someone has just called up
        your child
    specifically to tell him that he's *not*
        invited to the birthday party.
That's when we—whether we're single or
        married, alone or with much
        support—
    have to grasp Your grace, Lord,
    pull from Your strength,
    lean on Your love,
    and hang on for dear life!

Sitter Sagas

"Oh, Lord, I've got the sitters' blues!
It's *so* hard to find someone who will
      lovingly care for my sons
            when I have to be away.
And lately, with having to earn extra money
                  to make ends meet,
            it seems like I have to be away more
                  and more."

That was a song I sang quite often at the
                  beginning
      of being a single mom.
I've learned a lot about assertiveness by
            hiring sitters.
I've realized how naive I was, how trusting,
      but how far I've come.
I used to be taken in by how someone
            wanted to appear to me,
only to find that they'd spent the whole
            time on the phone
      or fussing at the boys or going outside
            to smoke.

Once, I was met at the door by an irate sitter
      who informed me that my boys were so
            badly behaved that
      she couldn't get them to sit down
            quietly in the waiting area

and keep their hands off the cigarette
machine.
When I asked what she was talking about,
she said she had *had* to get her car's
brakes worked on,
because by the time I got home in the
afternoon, it was too late.
I told her that I wouldn't even take my boys
to a brake place
to wait for a long time,
and she said it wasn't *that* long, just a
couple of hours.
Sean had taken his security jacket that he
called Jackie with him, left it, tried
to tell her, and had cried all the way
home.
When he told me, I quickly called the brake
place,
only to be told that it had been tossed
in the dumpster
as an old rag—it in fact looked like
one!—and that
the garbage truck was due any time.
The boys and I—the sitter had somewhere
else she *suddenly* needed to be—
raced over and joined a mechanic and
the owner in the dumpster,
where after forty-five minutes,
ruining my outfit,
having hands I questioned would ever
come clean,

and having to hold off the garbage truck,
we *finally* found it.
It was almost the same after I had washed it
      sixty-five times . . .

Another time, I got home to find three
      angry, upset boys
  who had been fed peanut butter and
      jelly sandwiches
  while they watched the sitter and her
      friend feast on
  pizza she'd had delivered after I left.

Still another sitter took the boys to her
      health club,
  checked them into *their* daycare,
  and set about her aerobics and weight
      work.
I discovered this after the boys casually
      mentioned
  going to the "club" every day.
When I was furious, she couldn't see
      anything wrong
  with my paying her to work out
  while someone else took care of the boys!

I quickly became skeptical and careful
      about who watched my boys.
I instructed more, gave more clear-cut
      expectations,
  let it be known in no uncertain terms
  what I simply would NOT tolerate.
I weeded out.

I was extremely selective, planned as far
    ahead as I could,
     and, despite my limited finances,
     paid them *really* well.
I was forced into placing boundaries around
    my family:
     to say we are worth the very best
      in consideration,
      in quality.
We are important people,
     if not in the world's eyes,
     in the eyes of our loving Father,
     who cares enough
     to get my sons the best care.

STEPPING IN GUM

Don't you hate it
   when you step in gum?

It's such a sticky mess,
   and what burns you up
   is that it was left by someone else
   and you just happened to step in it.

Now every step you take
   has a thwok sound—
      leather adhering to vinyl for a split
      second—
   slowing you down,
   making you crazy.

I stepped in a big wad years ago.
And I can't completely get it off my shoe:
   Sorry, you can't have a loan; your
      credit's bad.
   Your son has a learning disability,
      usually transmitted through the
      male gene.
      Did your ex-husband have similar
      difficulty?
   I'm sorry, we cannot take your check.
      The computer says a check
      from six years ago was never taken
      care of.

I never told you this before, I was afraid
     it would embarrass you,
          but your ex-husband said . . .

Don't you hate it
     when you step in gum?

You end up sticky
     for life, it seems.

Checks That Go Back

There should be a law against
   checks that go back.

Checks that are taken back out of accounts
   and then mess up the balance
   so that other checks
                  written for groceries,
                  water bills,
                  and braces
                           go back too!

There should be some way of telling if
         they'll bounce
   before you deposit them.

There should be some way of no longer
         believing,
                  no longer hoping,
                           that someone
                           can change.

There should be a law against being this
         trusting,
                           this naive,

         I think;

   as I stand here
   with yet another

      returned check

            in my outstretched
            hand.

YOU KNOW HOW I LOVE CLOSURE, LORD

There's no closure with divorce when you
        have children.
And You know how I love closure, Lord.
With divorce
    there is visitation,
            the getting packed for it,
            the aftermath of tired tantrums,
            the settling back into a routine,
            only to be disrupted in another two
            weeks' time.
    There are phone calls
            at inopportune times.
    There are Game Gears that come in the
            mail on a rainy day
            after you have said no, they're too
            expensive.
    There is anger.
    There is feeling sick and tired of being a
            pawn in this game
            you don't want to play.

Never does the Bible say, "Blessed are the
            divorcees,"
            the victims, the ones laid waste
            from another's life of
                self-indulgence.

I know You love the boys and me.

I'm sure You are keeping us in Your care.
But, Lord, when am I going to experience
that blessed closure?
You know how I love closure.

Thanksgiving I

This year I'm doing it right!
Thanksgiving in style—
        a regular Norman Rockwell portrait.
The whole turkey-stuffing-mashed potatoes-
        cranberry sauce schmear.

I use every pot, every pan, every dish.
My best table linens grace our table.
The food is primo—
        meant to assuage all the guilt for those
                multitude of
                        fast food/cereal dinners our frantic
                        lifestyle requires.

Here, at long last, is a meal to be truly savored,
                                lingered over,
                                        appreciated.

"What is this stuff?"
"Oooo, yuck! Do I have to eat this?"
"Where's the Kraft macaroni and cheese?"
"Can I just have Spiderman pasta?"

I fold up my napkin,
        placing it gently by my plate.
I know when I'm beat.

"Boys," I smile at them, "let's go see
        Aladdin."

They look at me wide-eyed,
    waiting for the irritated lecture.
Surprisingly, it doesn't come.

Instead, by God's grace,
    I am able to stand and walk away
        with the poise of a dancer
    from the table flowing over with the
        bounty of
        $74.56 worth of "what's thats."

I don't dare look back.

MY PITCHING'S GETTING BETTER, LORD

My pitching's getting better, Lord!
My sons grin at me
> as more balls find their way
> over the plate,
> and the impatience of, "That's
> okay, Mom, try it again,"
> becomes the exuberance of, "All
> right, Mom, you GOT one!"

We stand in the weed-infested, scraggly
> front yard,
> a little cluster of four:
>> three little guys with baseball
>> caps and big dreams
>> and one woman pitching her
>> heart out.
It's so obvious to the elderly couple waving
> in the blue car
> that daily rounds our corner,
> there is no man here.
Their eyes send out sympathy and strength,
> a combination something like,
>> "That's right! Go get 'em,
>>> you poor sweet darling with
>>> those three little boys.
>>> Bless your heart . . . "
I feel it.

At the grocery store, at church, at their
        soccer games, at the movies,
    but more
    when the four of us go out to dinner,
    and the hostess looks behind us and asks,
        "Will there be five? Or only four . . . ?"

The unspoken question remains,
    "Bless your heart, what happened?"
A perky blonde woman, feminine, sweet,
        soft-spoken,
        "saddled" with three boys—
           boisterous, restless, and wild.

How could they know
    that these boys are the joy and focus of
        my life,
    just as they are my pain and my burden
        sometimes?
They pull me forward—
    my momentum.

And without them,
    who knows
    if my pitching would *ever* have
           gotten better!

"That's It!"

Palm trees,
    bold, brown palm trees
    on dark grass-cloth wallpaper,
just didn't cut it
as a backdrop
for my rice-carved, four-poster bed.

They stood out in glaring contrast to
gleaming cherry wood
spread with stripes of dusky rose, sea-foam
      green,
    cream, and soft terra-cotta.
The small pillows placed carefully against
    the bolsters
seemed to whisper, "Save us! We can't take
    it anymore!"

So, one night, I said, "That's it!"
I stood on my bed barefooted
    and began gingerly peeling back a
    corner of the wallpaper.
Tentative, tenderly I began;
then I was amazed at how easily it parted
    from the wall,
    almost as if it was as relieved to *be* off
    the wall
    as I was to *get* it off.
I began ripping it off,

73

sheets at a time.
It fairly *flew* off.
I hollered for joy.

Sean stood transfixed in my bedroom
                doorway.
The look on his face telling me he had
                decided that *this* time
        Mom had really flipped out.
"Come on up, Sean!" I crowed. "Join in!"
Disbelieving, but quickly, before I came to
                my senses,
        he was on the bed in one leap.
Squealing, pulling, ripping,
        hooting with joy and release.

Together we were yanking down the gross,
        the unacceptable, the we're-not-gonna-
                take-this-anymore
and replacing it with this-is-where-we-are-
                today.

I would later have a color specially mixed to
                exactly match
        the soft terra-cotta stripe of my
                comforter;
and as I rolled it on, I would feel such a
                deep joy
        that it would spread through me,
        filling my very fingertips.

But *no* feeling can quite compare
to that glorious tearing off of the palm trees!

Me, who opens wrapped gifts so
        painstakingly slow that
   it frustrates all those around me,
ripping that paper from the wall,
sharing Sean's exuberance and delight and
        wonder!

A slow, rich chuckle rumbled up
   from the soles of my bare feet that night
and flew up to land on my bedroom ceiling,
where it remains
        to this day.

COLLECTING
DIVORCED MEN

The light flashes on the answering
        machine.
Pushing the button, I hear Donny's voice,
                followed by Benny's,
                followed by Tom's, Bobby's,
                Steve's,
                and then Brian's.

I seem to be collecting them.
Divorced men.
I don't know where they're all coming from.
They just appear overnight.
Like plaque, they come with sweetness.
They're so generous.
They offer to take the boys and me to
                movies, to the mountains to get
                apples,
        out to dinner.
But I've learned,
there is always a cost to me.

Once, dinner was on Benny.
But dinner ended up being an hour away
                because of a coupon he had,
        and the wait at the restaurant was
                another hour.
I don't know if it was the frustration of
                maintaining the boys' behavior

or the constant pumping of the gas
    pedal on the way back,
but I arrived home with a sick headache
    and a queasy stomach.
Three boys had passed tired two hours ago,
    and it was eleven o'clock on a
    school night.
Benny may have picked up the tab,
    but I paid, big time, for that one.

Roses appeared on my desk at school.
My third graders were all aflutter, wondering
    who sent them.
I knew.
I had received similar ones the afternoon
    before
    and would probably get some more
    later on in the week.
Free? Not really.
They were followed by lingering drop-in visits,
    by three or four phone calls,
        during the long-awaited, so-precious-to-
        me evening hours alone.

The thoughtfulness is touching.
Really.
I just wish the price tag wasn't expectations.

I like them. They're funny, warm, comfort-
    able to be with.
The boys like them too. They lap up their
    maleness like warm milk.
But when I invite one to share our Easter

77

egg hunt
or another to join in our birthday
celebration,
they seem to take that as an invitation to
join the family.
They see in me—I don't know—something
that attracts them.
Something that helps them get through
another day alone.

They want more than friendship from me.
"Donny's in love with you," my eight-year-
old Sean pronounces.
"But you don't love him, I can tell."
How is he able to see what Donny can't
or won't?
That magical, mystical something is missing.
I can't manufacture it,
won't fake it,
refuse to settle
for anything less than WOW!
I've settled for back-row tickets
when there were no other ones available,
and back was better than nothing;
a stain on a purple linen jacket
when the store takes another
30 percent off;
even scraping mayonnaise off my hamburger
when we're in a hurry and there's no
time to reorder.
But I *will not* settle for convenience,
"the feelings may come,"

"at least he doesn't drink,
smoke, or gamble."
I want *wonderful*!
I want *magnificent*!

And I'll tell you something else:

I'm willing to wait.

My, You Have Your Hands Full

I'd be a millionaire today
if I had just a dollar for each time someone
    has told me
        "Oh, my! You have your hands full!"
"Three boys!" they say,
as if they could substitute *boa constrictors*
    and not change the meaning.
"Oh, my! How do you do it?"
"Very nicely," I hope my smile says.
"With God's help and a great sense of humor,"
    I want to say.

You *have* to find humor
    somehow
in your dryer breaking in January
    with no money to buy a new one,
    even on payday!

So you name the mountain of dirty clothes
        you've all created,
and you learn to prioritize
    by picking the five most important pieces
    to take over to your friend's house to
        wash and dry.
You praise God
    for friends like that,
and then you go on
    to the next crisis.

TIME FOR ME

Okay.
Let's see—
> I bought the pizza.
> Called to recheck with the sitter.
> She's coming at 6:00.

Sean will be delivered back here at 6:30
> after soccer.
Neil will be picked up at 7:00 for his
> practice and brought back afterward.
I've written the note about who has
> homework and left the three sets of
> spelling words on the refrigerator.
Jeff needs to take these two pills before he
> goes to bed.
Neil's pills are right there.

Drinks? Oh, yes, there's Sprite in the
> refrigerator.
I must remember to tell her no Coke
> because of the caffeine.
Maybe it'd just be easier to take the Coke
> out and hide it.
But she may want Coke.

My racket? Okay, there it is, but I can find
> only one of my Thorlo socks.
Maybe the other one's still in the dryer.

Or maybe it got mixed in with the boys'!
Balls, visor, yeah, two shoes! No time to
      scrounge for those.

Where are we playing tonight?
I wrote the directions down somewhere . . .
On the back of a pink envelope, I think.
Or was it yellow?

Ah, here's the sitter.
What?
Oh, thanks! My water bottle, I almost forgot.
Bye now! There's pizza!
Remember bedtime at 8:30! I left a note
      about homework!
Whoops—where's my racket? Oh, over my
      shoulder.

Well . . . I'm off!
To relax.
To take time for me.
I just wish
I wasn't so exhausted!

Toy Soldiers

I AM GOING TO KILL HIM!
How many times have I told him to put
          away ALL those little green
     plastic soldiers?
Does *anything* hurt worse than to have your
          heel come down
     on their artillery weapons, held up at
          the ready position,
          or their uniquely posed SHARP elbows
          and knees?
They hide in the carpet and attack at
          sundown.
Their aim: mother's bare feet.

How could something so small cause so
          much pain?
Why didn't I see it coming?
How many *more* are there, scattered around,
          hidden,
     to be found with their individual stabs
     by my thin skin?

It's like life, Lord.
There are so many "little" things hidden,
          waiting to "get us," to cause us pain.
And somehow, I torture myself with the
          mistaken notion
     that I should have been able to see it
          coming.

83

But how could I possibly have done that?
Surely You have tried to tell me all these years
    that I am not God,
      that there is no way I can foresee or
        even discern everything,
      that it is indeed by hindsight that we
        humanly learn!

Perhaps it is better to "arm" myself with
      slippers
    than to kick myself for not seeing the
      unseeable.

WAITING FOR THE ANSWERS

I feel numb, Lord.
No, more like mixed-up.
My heart has doubled over itself in a square
 knot:
 right over need, and need over right.
Part of me wants to get this decided,
 all sewed up in a neat little package.
And part of me is saying,
 "Hey, wait a minute here. This is my *life*
 you're talking about."
This relationship is going too fast, and I feel
 panicky.
I want to know *right now*,
 and I want to take all the time I need.
I wish I had Your vision, God;
 I'm so tired of making mistakes and
 seeing them in hindsight!
Help me slow down and breathe in Your
 Spirit of wisdom.
If I don't know what to do, help me have
 the strength and the willpower
 to do nothing,
 to stay put,
 to make no sudden moves,
 to have faith,

 and wait
 for the answers.

LEARNING TO RECEIVE

"Do not worry then, saying, 'What will we
eat?' or 'What will we drink?' or 'What
will we wear for clothing?' . . . For your
heavenly Father knows that you need all
these things. But seek first His kingdom
and His righteousness, and all these
things will be added to you. So do not
worry about tomorrow; for tomorrow will
care for itself. Each day has enough trouble of its own." (Matt. 6:31-34)

How do You know, Father, when I'm at my
        absolute last ounce of strength?
When I'm ready to throw in the towel and
        say, "You win, world!
    You're right; a single mother of three
        boys
    cannot make it on a teacher's salary."
When I have the boys' conferences, all three
        in a row,
    and each teacher tells me each son
        needs *more* help from me,
    more structure from me, more of my
        time.
When I balance my checkbook and discover
        that, once again,
    if it weren't for my paycheck being

86

automatically deposited
one day before payday, I'd be overdrawn.
When it's soccer sign-up time again;
    it's fifty dollars a child,
    plus they each need new soccer shoes
        and shorts,
    at the same time all three have
        outgrown
        their regular shoes
        and their jeans.

How do You sense, Father,
    that I so need a lift?
How do You alert others to send that lift,
    to come forward with loving offers?
Judy offering to take the boys for Happy
        Meals while I work late at school.
Bobby asking if he can help by taking Sean
        to and from his soccer practices.
An anonymous fifty dollar Kroger gift
        certificate left on my desk
    near the end of the month.
Pam having the boys spend the night when
        I was coming down with bronchitis
    and needed some sleep.
A neighbor replacing the brakes on my car.
Bags of beautiful clothes for the boys brought
        to my house, to my classroom.

Oh, Father, the Giver of all good things,
    I am so grateful.
Thank You for all these love-filled gifts.

Thank You for the wonderful people who
      bring them,
    whom You choose to work through.
And, Lord, through these acts of generous
      kindness,
    I am learning one of the hardest lessons
      of my life:
      how to receive.

It's more fun to give,
    to wrap up the presents
    and watch the faces light up with delight.
Giving can be a rush, an empowering
      experience.

Receiving humbles me.
It makes me vulnerable,
    in a position where I'm beholden to
      another,
    where I need someone else.
It's *scary* to receive;
    but, You know, Lord,
    now that I've had to learn to receive
      from people,
    maybe I have a tiny bit more
      understanding
    about how to receive from You.
Possibly, it's opened me up
    to receiving all that You desire to give me.
And, oh, glorious Father,
    I know You have the absolute *best* for me.
    Thank You.

I Believe in Your
Angels, Lord

Lord, I believe in Your angels.
I know the boys' and mine work overtime.
They go with us the eighteen hundred miles
        on the highway to Kansas City.
They fly above the boys as they venture on
        weekends with their dad.
They soothe my soul as I worry about his
        judgment.
They hover over the three of them as they
        play street hockey with wild abandon,
            roller blade down hills,
            leap over creeks,
            climb trees that are way too tall.
They rest gently at their bedsides as their
        sleep-heavy eyelids
            fight to stay awake.

I've named them.
    Mine's Gladys.
    Sean's is Clarence.
    Neil's is Jacob.
    And Jeff's is Charlie.

We met Charlie, I'm sure of it.

One day, we went to the track to run.
We were preparing for a one-mile Fun Run
        at the Square,
        and Jeff wouldn't run.

With his chin stuck out stubbornly, he said,
    "No way!"
      and crossed his arms as he closed his
      heart.
Sean, Neil, and I began running laps.
I kept my eye on Jeff, and suddenly I saw a
      man in a red shirt and blue jeans
      holding a can of paint and a brush.
He asked Jeff why he wouldn't run.
He told him how good it would make him
      feel
      as he brushed the paint back and forth,
      back and forth
      on the metal railing of the stadium.
Where the brush moved,
    Jeff's eyes followed.
Charlie said to him, "Tell you what, Jeff.
    You go run three laps,
    and I'll let you paint."
In a flash, Jeff was out on the track, eyes
      sparkling, legs pumping.
Then he was back at the railing, painting
      with Charlie,
      telling him he was afraid to run
      Saturday,
      as the brushes pushed the paint back
      and forth, back and forth.

What Charlie told him,
    I'll never know.
But he instilled courage and confidence in
    Jeff.

Gave him wings of an eagle
    as he flew to a seven-minute finish that
        Saturday.
Spurred him on to race away fear,
    to run away doubt,
    to finish.

And, Charlie, if you're listening,

        Jeff hasn't stopped yet!

THANKSGIVING II

Okay, now, this year we've truly got it:
　　　the big idea.

Let's go out to eat for Thanksgiving.

No shopping and chopping,
　　boiling and basting,
only to have no one
　　willing to do the tasting.
No sir!
We're going out!

All dressed up, we head out—
　　spirits highs, mouths watering.
So much to choose from in Atlanta's
　　　awesome array
　　of culinary treats.

Something should have told me to go
　　　downtown
　　or make reservations
　　or at least call ahead.

Imagine our surprise when the first fifty
　　　places we chugged up to
　　were closed!

"Mom, the gas says E again!"
Not a gas station in sight.
Oh, great, we're going to end up stranded

on the side of the road
on Thanksgiving,
starving
and scared.
Not exactly the picture of Plymouth Rock.

Ah, but look yonder, on the horizon.
Land ho!
Hope cometh in the name of
the Black-Eyed Pea Restaurant,
where we feast upon the traditional fare
of
corn dogs,
chicken fingers,
and love.

OUT OF CONTROL

I heard a crash, followed by a muffled gasp,
and then
      silence.
What in the world? I thought as I stopped,
    mascara wand paused midair.
Better go check.
I was totally unprepared for what met my eyes.

There was Neil,
    at the bottom of the nine steps
    that led up to the bedrooms,
    struggling to upright his brand-new
      bicycle.
The front wheel was off the ground and
      spinning wildly.
He was trying to lift and turn and straighten
    all at the same time.
The expression on his face was a curious
      and unique blend
    of panic, surprise, thinly masked
      delight, and shock.
When he heard me say his name,
    his head snapped around,
    and the looks were totally replaced
    with panic and fear.
Before I could even get one syllable out of
      my mouth,
    Neil was talking eighty miles per hour,

trying to explain his way
out of this mess.
The day before had been his birthday,
and he had wanted a new bike more
than anything.
My parents had sent the money, and he got
to pick it out.
We paid Toys R Us—not being fools—to
put it together,
and we had gone over to pick it up last
night.
Apparently, Neil had decided to have it
"spend the night"
with him for just one night,
was successful going *up* the stairs the
night before,
but when he was trying to get it back
down,
it got out of control
and *flew* down the stairs.
"Wow, Mom, you shoulda seen that baby
go!" Neil exclaimed.

His brothers gathered around, amazed, but
then not amazed
at another of Neil's antics.
This is the kid who
scurries up twenty-foot trees
like a monkey
and is fearless.
I was just thinking that we better get a
move on

to get to school on time,
when I looked down as Neil moved his
    bike back
and saw that the corner of my writing
    desk
        had been taken clean off.
I don't remember much about the next few
    minutes,
    except that I saw blinding white
    and felt such utter rage
    that I totally lost control.
I started crying, then screaming,
    then I grabbed Neil by the shoulders
    and shook him.
He started crying, along with Jeff,
        and Sean stood there
        horrified.
It was as if that desk were some sort of
    symbol for
    all that I'd lost: my house, my credit
        rating, my pride, my diamond,
        my neighborhood,
        my happily-ever-after.
I looked at that desk,
    and I can say, that's the *only* thing
        that mattered
    for two minutes.
Then I looked at my three scared—
        more like freaked-out—
    sons, and I melted.
Different tears rolled down my cheeks
    as I asked for their forgiveness.

I held them close, and we all cried.
One of them said we'd probably be late, and
          someone else said,
     "So what else is new?"
We all laughed through our tears.

I don't remember now if we were late for
          school that day.
In the great scheme of things, it doesn't
          really matter.
What does matter is that people and feelings
          and my family
     will forevermore come before things.

DATING WITH CHILDREN

A classy guy:
>   He had presence,
>   dignity,
>   panache.

I had dressed in sequins, silk, and pearls
>   for his black tie affair.
We had gone to jazz dinner clubs, plays,
>   elegant restaurants.

So what in heaven's name were we doing
>   sitting in Sonny's Bar-B-Que,
>   trying to tame my three sons—
>   who seemed *determined* on destroying
>   any semblance of a lasting
>   relationship?

"Why'd we have to come here?" one of them
>   pipes.
"Hey, you're kinda bald," sweet talks another.
"What happened to your finger?" chirps the
>   third. "It get cut off or something?"

I want to die.

One spills his Coke.
The other refuses to eat his grilled cheese.
>   "It's yucky, Mom; they used the wrong
>   kind of cheese."

"Do you have a pool?" chimes in "Helpful
        Harry." "Mom's other boyfriend had
        a pool.
    With a diving board."

I want to throttle them.
I want to go home.
I want to start this night over.
Or skip it completely.

A straw sword fight breaks out across the
        table.
I separate, to try to conquer,
    and march one Musketeer
    to his own private table,
    where he sits and sulks
    until, ah, sweet deliverance,
        it's time at last to go home.

Thank you!
Are we having fun yet?
So much for the world of dating
                with children.

MY SLEEK, TAN DOLPHINS

When things get really bad,
when I've been late for work the last four
      out of five mornings
    and been caught without lesson plans *again*
    (why don't they ever check when mine
      are detailed,
      complete, and ready?),
when I'm bone tired and tempted to feel
      sorry for myself,
all I have to do
    is close my eyes
and think about
    jumping in those foamy Florida waves
    with my boys.

We went to the beach that summer with
      friends,
    another family we tried to mix with.
Sometimes it worked, sometimes it didn't
    (like any time their daughter
    was anywhere around *any* of my sons).
So we split up and did our own thing
      during part of the days.
And my thing
    was jumping in the waves.

I had jumped waves as a young girl on the
    New Jersey shore.

It was one of my fondest memories.
Somehow, when I grabbed the hands of my
      three sons
    and went flying down toward the surf,
I had come full circle.

I was the mom
    watching *my* children giggle
    as the waves tossed and played
    with them.
They were seven, five, and three.
Sweet ages, when they don't yet object
    to holding their mom's hand in public.
And they played in those waves
    like sleek, tan dolphins.

When the electric bill is sky-high
    and the checking account is low,
when the three sets of homework
    add up to more hours
    than we have until bed,
when I'm all settled and ready for my
      favorite TV show
    only to turn it on and find it's been
      preempted
    for a documentary on war-torn Romania,
I close my eyes,
    hear the pounding surf,
    smell the salty/suntan lotion scent,
    and take a little jump
    in the waves
      caught forever in my mind.

THE FIRST SMALL
STEP AFTER PANIC

Lord, my friend Lisa Short died today.
She was only thirty-six.
She was diagnosed with cancer five
      months ago.
It went so fast:
    the cancer and our friendship.
We had just found each other a year ago.
We grew so close very quickly.
We had traveled down some of the same
      paths—
    divorce, men who had robbed us of our
      dignity,
    rebuilding, peace, single parenthood.
We laughed through our tears
    as we rocked on her porch swing.
We'd tell "I can top that" stories of hardships,
    embarrassments, and triumphs.
We held each other softly in hugs
    of total acceptance
    and trust.
She had one son, I had my three, and we'd
      swap
    little boy stories and offer advice,
      solutions,
    to ongoing or new problems.

My sons knew she was dying.

They loved her too, so they were sad and
        confused.
The questions they asked were endless.
I answered them the best I could.
But the one question that really threw me,
        Lord,
was the one Sean asked me for all three of
        them:
"Mom, what do we do if *you* die?"
I gathered them to me, a hen shielding her
        chicks,
    and explained how much my parents,
        my brother, and my sister loved them.
I told them how much their father and his
        parents loved them.
"There will be so many people to love you
        and care for you," I said.
"No, Mom, *no*," Sean said impatiently, "I
        mean, what do we do first?"
Then it dawned on me that Lisa had died at
        home.
Were my three wondering what they would
        do immediately
    if they found me dead?

One look at their three huge sets of somber
        eyes told me yes.
"Well," I said calmly. "You would go to the
        phone and call
    Mr. and Mrs. Osborne
    or Mr. and Mrs. Dean
    or Mr. and Mrs. Cagle.

Let's go downstairs and look up their
            numbers and write them
        in a special place by our phone,
            so you'll know where they are.
We can even practice dialing them now, if
            you'd like."
We trooped down the stairs, a serious band,
            and completed the task.
We discussed what they could say and if
            they should dial 911.
I asked if they had more concerns; anything
            else they wanted to discuss.
"Nope!" they said and smilingly asked if
            they could go out and play now.
In shock, I said, "Sure, why not?"
        and watched their vanishing backs
            as I heard
        their playful chatter and whoops.

Wow, Lord!
They just wanted the first step.
They didn't want to know who they would
            live with,
        what would happen to the stuff in their
            bedrooms,
        or who would pay for their college!
They simply wanted directions for that first
            tiny moment of panic.
The moment they lost their security: me.

Please help me be more like them in that way.
To ask You for, and be satisfied with,

the first step,
the very next thing,
instead of planning out and worrying about
all that lies ahead,
all the uncertainty.

Five months and a day ago,
I had no idea I'd be saying good-bye to Lisa.
I just knew she was my special friend,
and that was enough.

Receipts

Where *are* they? I thought as the papers
        went flying out of the box
  in the bottom of my closet.

I *know* I saw the one from the shoe store a
        couple of days ago
    and the one from the department store
    last week!

I *need* those receipts!

It was happening again.
Broke time.
Time to take back the unworn, the unused,
    the frivolous, bought-on-the-spur-of-
        the-moment things.
The things for me.
The feel-goods.
The little indulgences that caused me to
    whisper, "I'm worth it."

But there never seemed to be enough
        money for those and
  the things we really need,
      like lights and water and gas for
      the car.

Oh well, I think, if I can just find those
    receipts and take this stuff back,

then maybe next month or the month
    after that
I can get new lacy underwear or
    sweet silky lotion for my dry legs.

The important thing today is that we eat
    and that we can see to eat.
So, since the electricity bill is due tomorrow
    and the paycheck's not for another two
       weeks,
I'll look and look for those receipts
    and face the humiliation of those
       customer service clerks
    who ask so unfeelingly, '"Was there
       anything *wrong* with it ma'am?"
I'll trade my momentary hot cheeks
    for cash in the hand
    and peace in my mind
       that we've made it
          for another month.

THE CONFERENCE

My hands were clenched in balls of rage;
thumbnails tearing at the sides of the other
    nails,
    gouging away pieces of myself,
just as this parent's words being spat at me
    scooped out portions of my dignity,
    carved away sections of my hard-won
        worth.
I composed myself, trying not to show the
        pounding of my head,
    the dryness of my throat, the loss of
        pride.
Who was this woman to judge me?
Had she walked where I had?
Forget her. Disregard her. Pay her no mind.
Don't let her determine who you are, I told
        myself.
Don't let her put a price on your value.
No one knows what you intended. No one
        knows your heart, your very soul.
The pouring out of who you are into what
        you do.
The intensity, the totality of your offering.
That it consumes you just as it defines you.
Empties you as it refills and refuels your spirit.

Who was this person to try to take away

what I was?
To belittle me by charting the progress I
made in others' lives?
To make me justify and explain the *whys*
and *hows*
of what I do
out of sheer love?

I straightened my steel backbone and held
my chin steady
as I walked with dignity out of the
office
and back to my classroom.
Back to the children who rip me apart
just as they incredibly add more
and more layers to my heart,
back to the place that is both
excruciatingly hard
and laughingly easy,
back to the place that has defined me
and left me limitless
from the moment I first entered it,
back to who I know I am.
This time, more determined than ever
not to doubt it again.

BROTHER GERMS

They all three had the same, you know—
it was decided among them.
You couldn't catch anything real bad
     from drinking from your *brother's* cup.
I mean, how else are you going to share one
          large drink
     everywhere we go?
          Movies, McDonalds, the zoo.

Hey, who bit the straw again!

Brother germs make it all okay.
They came to terms with it.
So much so
     that when my friend Pam Dean took
          them to a movie
     and they each got their own drink,
                    they didn't know what
                    to do.

"Oh, Lisa," she said, "that's so sad . . ."

No, I thought, it's called
                    survival.

DEEP DREAMS

When I get into a really deep sleep,
    I have these dreams, Lord.

I'm caught in an elevator that keeps going
            up and down
        in a dorm or a hotel.
The doors open on each floor, and, no,
            that's not the floor I want.
I can't find the right floor.
And so I travel floor to floor all night long.

Sometimes it's the first day of school,
        and I can't find my classroom
        or I don't know which grade I'm teaching
        or my classroom is not set up, and I'm
            running around
            frantically searching for supplies
            and materials so that I can teach.

And then there's the day-of-the-big-exam-
            and-I-haven't-studied dream.
I'm panicked and desperate and can't believe
        I forgot all about this major test.
        It's horrible and so real that I'm always
            stunned
            when I wake up and realize it was
            only a dream.

What is my mind trying to tell me, Lord?

That I'm overloaded and stressed out?
Or is it perhaps seeking peace for past choices
    that ended up being mistakes?
Why do these dreams take so much out
      of me?
Why do they seem so real and keep repeating?

I hand them over to You, Lord,
    the great Unraveler.
Help me find peace in my sleep
    instead of adding more chaos
    to a life that is already filled with it.
Help me, Lord,
        to rest . . .

Flying Plastic Hamburgers and Squirt Guns in the House

Just the other day, Lord,
    I was in my room doing something, I
        can't remember what now,
when all of a sudden it hit me that it was
        too quiet.
Uh-oh, I thought, that usually means
        something
    that I'd *rather* not know about is going on,
    and I'd better go investigate
    before I'm sorry.

As I rounded the corner, I heard the
        strangest sound.
It was a swishing-type noise, similar to milk
        hitting the inside of the bucket
    when a cow is being milked.
I stopped dead in my tracks.
There were Neil and Jeff: Neil standing at
        the top of the stairs;
    Jeff sitting at the bottom holding a giant
        red balloon.
Neil had a water gun, and he was squirting
        the balloon in constant,
    rhythmic swishes.
Jeff was grinning from ear to ear but,
        amazingly, not making a sound.
The water was jumping off the balloon,

113

splattering not only Jeff
but the silk flowers, the books, the
hardwood floor, the wallpaper.
I stood there, a fish with gaping mouth.
Surely they *sensed* rather then heard my
presence.
The water stopped, and the eyes got large.
"Give me gun. Get towels. Clean up. Go
rooms," I sputtered, Tarzan-style.
They ran around like scared rabbits.
If I hadn't been so mad, it would have been
funny.

Later, I was reminded of a much different
discovery.
That time, years ago, it had been the
amount of noise that had
summoned me.
All three boys had been in the playroom,
laughing, calling out to one another,
obviously on some kind of imaginative
adventure.
I reveled in their creativity and delight.
Peeking in, I was delighted that they were
gathered around
their Little Tikes kitchen.
Oh, that albatross that had hung around my
Santa neck
for four long months since Christmas!
Why ever had I thought that, just because I
had to *pry* their fingers
away from any Little Tikes kitchen at

          any friend's house,
     they would even in the least like their
          own, or attempt to play with it,
     I don't know!

Well they hadn't played with it—another
          Christmas good intention gone
          bad—
     and every time I looked at it, I felt the
          frustration that always goes with
     missing the mark.
But now—glimmer of hope—perhaps they
          had realized
     the error of their ways,
     and they would start cooking!

As the noise level escalated, so did my
          curiosity,
     until, finally, unable to hold myself back
          any longer,
     I quietly opened the door an inch and
          peered in.
Surely, I was not prepared for what I saw
          that time either!
They were playing with their kitchen, all
          right,
     but not in what you would call the
          traditional—or usual—way.
The kitchen was upside-down,
          with all three boys on top of it.
One's legs were stuck in the opened cabinet
          below the sink.

One wore the coffee pot as a hat.
They were all three hurling plastic
        hamburgers
    at some unseen enemies,
    whooping it up,
    having the time of their lives.

Both incidents taught me some lessons.

First, things are not always what they seem,
    especially when children and noise
        levels are involved.
Second, as a parent, I have expectations for
        my children.
Some are valid, like not shooting water guns
        in the house
    and respecting property.
Some call for reexamination, like wanting
        the boys to play with the kitchen
    as justification that I didn't make a
        mistake in my choice for them.

There's an element of surprise in both lessons.
Surprise that resulted in delight and discovery
    about them
        and me.

No Backup

One of the hardest things
    about being a single mom
    is that there is no backup.

No backup if you're sick,
                tired,
                have a headache,
                feel PMSy.

No backup on discipline,
                decisions,
                details,
                dilemmas.

Not when you're waiting
                at restaurants,
                in church,
                in movie theaters,
                at doctors' offices,
                in any line
                for anything.

No backup for tag-teaming,
                energy replenishment,
                peace of mind repair,
                soul cell replacement.

You want to yell,
                "Send in the relief pitcher!"

Lisa Hussey

"Where's the pinch hitter?"

Ah, but then it dawns on you:
  He is there all the time.

And three balls, two strikes
    are His specialty.

CONSIDER IT ALL JOY

Consider it all joy, my brethren, when
you encounter various trials, knowing that
the testing of your faith produces
endurance. (James 1:2–3)

Joy?
Was James kidding?
Consider it *joy* when you hit the hard times?
What if they seem like one continuous,
        never-ending hard time?
What then, James?

I was thinking these thoughts, sitting at my
        desk one day after school
    as I gazed at the Scripture taped onto
        the wall beside me.
It had been a bad week.
Neil's soccer coach had told me that Neil
        had an "attitude problem,"
    and had I ever thought about spending
        more time with him
    and doing things that would bring up
        his self-esteem?
"Mister," I wanted to say, "that's what I've
        been working on with Neil for years.
    In fact, my other two sons tell me I
        spend too much time with Neil,
    and *they* want more of my time!"

I'd had a parent greet me at my classroom
        door this morning,
        demanding that her child's seat be
        switched in the seating chart.
I forgot my carefully prepared salad on the
        countertop at home,
        and the choices for lunch were bologna
        sandwiches with watery coleslaw
        and spaghetti pie.
The boys and I were late—again—and ran
        smack into the principal
        on our way in.
I felt like crying or ripping down that
        Scripture or both that afternoon,
        when my classroom door opened
        and in walked a young man.

The first thing I remember about Matt
        was his calm, his quiet purposefulness.
He was there to do a job, and he did it.
He did it with dignity, which is not easily
        done when you're doing custodial
        work,
        but without a chip on his shoulder
        or an air of "I'm better than this."
I remember his quiet smile, his politeness,
        his whole manner that put me at ease
        and added to the end of each of my
        school days.
We began talking each afternoon.
I found out that he was working his way
        through college.

That he wanted to be either a policeman
       like his father
   or a lawyer.
That he had a heart for justice, a compassion
       for other people.
I told him about the summer during college
     that I had worked as a maid in a
        convention center,
     about the way people had treated me,
     from, "You're not the average maid!"
        and, "What's a nice girl like you
        doing in a place like this?"
     to, "You're doing menial labor, therefore
        you are scum," and, "Hey, girlie,
        get me more towels *now*!"
It was a common link, and he told me how
       some teachers spoke to him,
     how others were some of the nicest
       people he'd met.
He especially liked my close friend Judy.
We laughed and talked, growing more and
       more at ease with one another.
A warm, comfortable friendship evolved.

One day, he asked me about the three
       pictures on my desk.
So I told him about Sean, Neil, and Jeff.
When I didn't speak of a husband,
     he noticed, I'm sure, but he was too
       polite to ask.
Later, I figured he probably learned my
       situation from Judy,

because he just assumed I knew that he
    knew
    I was a single parent.
After awhile, he offered to come over some-
    time
    to throw the football with the boys
    or if I needed some time to myself
    or to run errands.
He kept saying he didn't know how I did it
    all by myself.
So, I finally took him up on his offer
    and asked him if he could watch the
        boys
    for a couple of hours while I went to
        my tennis lesson that next Monday.
I insisted on paying him; after all, he was
        working his way through school,
    and, single parent or not, I was
        gainfully employed.
And so it began: a wonderful series of
    Monday nights that went on
    through
    the fall into the winter, when I had to
    wear gloves to play tennis.
One Monday night, Matt arrived before we
    were finished eating dinner,
    and I said, "Grab a plate, there's plenty!"
He did, and that was the start of another
    Monday night ritual:
    having Matt over for dinner.
The five of us laughed through pasta, tacos,

pizza, and chicken tenders—
all that "guy stuff" mine love so much.
And they looked so forward to him coming
that they would hurry and get their
homework done
so he could teach them new wrestling
holds.
From others, not Matt, I learned
that he had been a champion wrestler at
the local high school
and that he was currently on the 4.0
Dean's List in college.
Ever humble, he never put on airs but
shared with us his warm, true self.
When I got home from tennis, he'd have the
boys in bed—rarely in pajamas,
and sometimes without teeth brushed,
but *always* radiantly happy
that Matt had come to spend time with
them.
I'd find him studying hard or dozing
but always willing to chitchat for a few
minutes,
and we began to tell each other of the
people we were dating.
He was the little brother I'd always wanted
but never had.

He shared with us his own family—his
warm, remarkable mother,
who took care of my boys for a full two-
week period

so I could teach another course,
his sister Norah, who also sat for the
boys and became like their big
sister,
his brother Kenneth and his father who
were great role models
and often welcomed my sons into
their home.

One young man, who, when he stepped
into my portable classroom
that fall afternoon,
brought with him so many blessings, so
much joy.

I witnessed the difference Matt Martin
made in our four lives
when he was willing to be used by You,
Lord.
Through him, You helped me endure
and taught me to look for the joy
even in one of *those* weeks.

LOSING JEFF

The doorbell rings, and the first trick-or-
 treater stands expectantly
 with bag open.
"Oh, my," I exclaim, "What do we have here?"
I shovel handfuls of candy into each waiting
 sack, smile, and wave at the parents
 standing guard protectively at the curb.
I close my door with a sigh.
Halloween would forever remind me of the
 day I almost lost Jeff.

We were at Sean's soccer game—
 one of the hundreds we'd been to at the
 same park,
 Wildhorse Creek.
It was a sunny autumn day,
 and I was enjoying talking to the many
 parents I knew
 from teaching their children and from
 my boys' soccer teams.
I kept a watchful eye out for Neil and Jeff,
 playing behind me on the climbing
 wall, the tires,
 and racing up and down the barren hill
 with the other brothers and sisters of
 players and
 collecting the good ol' Georgia red clay

as laundry challenges to their moms.
Several times, Jeff came running up to tell
        me something
    or to ask for a drink of water.
And each time, someone would tell me how
        cute he was.
He *was* cute, even though it wore thin on
        me when he tried to use it
    to get what he wanted.
But it was his coloring—rosy-cheeked, big
        brown eyes, blond hair—
        along with his chunky build (Fireplug, I
        called him),
        and his funny personality—so animated
        and excited, lisping all his s's—
        that really grabbed people and won him
        fans.

The game ended, the drinks were being
        passed out, Sean came over to ask me
    what I thought of his kicks.
I spotted Neil and motioned him over.
I shielded my eyes to look for Jeff.
"Where's Jeff?" I asked Neil lightly when he
        ran up.
"I dunno," he answered with a shrug.
I turned my head, looking at the perimeter
        of pine trees
    surrounding the soccer fields.
"Go check the bathroom," I asked Neil.
"Sean, run up to the concession stand, and
        if Jeff is there,

126

tell him to come back here!" I shouted.
Several of the parents turned their heads.
"Jeff?" they asked. "I just saw him . . ."
More parents began looking around them,
      calmly, nonchalantly.
"Nope, Mom, not in the bathroom,"
      reported Neil.
"Hey! Jeff's not at the concession stand,
      Mom!" yelled Sean.

In the blink of an eye, the mood changed.
The Crosses, Sean's coach and his wife,
      looked significantly at one another.
Diane, the wife, said, "I'll go over to the
      horse ring
   and see if he wandered up there."
Bobby, the coach, said, "I'll take Amanda
      and see if he's up
   at the far playground."
Sean called to some of his soccer buddies,
      "Hey, can you help me look for my little
      brother in the woods?"
Neil stood, frozen to his spot, and slowly,
      slowly looked up at me.
I tried to reveal on my face none of the wild
      thoughts running in my brain.
I don't know how successful I was.
Not very, I think.

Soon the woods and the surrounding areas
      were ringing with
     "JEFF, JEEEFFFFF," and I began to relive

every moment
of what had started out as an ordinary
Saturday morning.
I remembered waking him up and smelling
that distinctly "Jeff smell"—
the sleepy essence that clings to each of
my boy's sheets
after they've been in them awhile.
I remembered kissing his soft, plump cheeks,
and his enormous eyes opening up.
He always wakes up so happy,
in contrast to Sean, who wakes up
slowly, like me,
and Neil, who often wakes up in a blue
funk.

When did he disappear? Why didn't I watch
him more closely?
Just *who all* had said he was so cute?
Some of those people I didn't even know,
and looking around now,
I didn't see them anywhere.
My mind's voice said the unthinkable:
"Maybe someone took him."

I looked at my watch and realized the game
had been over almost an hour.
Suddenly, half-remembered snatches of
made-for-TV movies
came tumbling through my brain.
"In half an hour, your child could be in
the next county."

"If you don't find your child in the first
     hour, the chances are slim to none
     he or she will ever be recovered
     alive . . ."

Tears, the first I'd allowed,
     filled my eyes.
I turned to another mom from the soccer
     team and asked,
       "How long do you wait before calling
       the police?"
       as calmly as I would have asked what
       degree oven
       and how many minutes when learning a
       new recipe.

Her eyes filled with tears more quickly than
     mine had.
She grabbed me in a fierce hug and hoarsely
     whispered, "Bless your heart,"
     into my shaking ear.
The dam broke.
Torrents of tears streamed down my face.
My shoulders shook.

The parents who had returned from their
     futile searches
     spoke strength to me with their eyes.
Some shuffled their feet and looked down.
I swallowed and, in one instant, got it
     together.
The crying stopped, the iron will I

depended on
to get me through crises returned.

But, amazingly, the fervent, steady prayers
prayed in strength and peace
quickly deteriorated into the bargain-
basement variety.
"Please, Lord, let me have my Jeff back," I
prayed.
"I promise to be more patient with him
when he takes forever to get out of
the car.
I'll never let him out of my sight.
Let me have one more chance . . ."

And then
the cry I'll never forget
rang out over that clear October
Atlanta air:
"WE FOUND HIM!"
"Lisa, we found him! In the woods.
Scrunched up. Hiding.
He thought he was going to get in trouble,
so he didn't answer when he heard us
call . . ."

Oh, praise God, they found him.
Never was my son more precious
than when I took his scared little face
between my shaking hands and said,
"Thank You, God!
Thank You, God!"

His big eyes took in my tears, the crowd
       around us, the noise, the relief.
And he said,
    "I'm in BIG trouble, aren't I?"

IN A CAST

Today at school, one of my students broke
    his arm.

And I realized that I have been a broken
    bone, Lord.
Shattered by cruel words spoken in anger,
    by shame that piled up and bowed me
        till I broke.
Crushed beneath the weight of finances
        gone wrong,
    children with special needs,
    a husband battling his own demons.
Smashed by decisions that *had* to be made.

And You, in Your love for me,
    have put me in a cast to heal.
For five years now
    You have cushioned me,
    protected me,
    held me still
        when I wanted to wiggle, fidget,
        and squirm.
You've held me close to You, Lord,
    so that in my very marrow
    I could become strong again.
Strong, to face whatever lies ahead in the
    lives of the boys,
    to make wise, timely decisions that are

based on Your truth.
Oh, there have been some bumps and bangs
along the way,
people and events that have delayed the
healing.
But despite any setbacks, Your healing
progresses to this day.
Your perfect love
that casts out fear.

It's Not So Bad, Really

"Lucky you," my friend said as we both
        headed to our cars
    after a faculty meeting that had lasted
        way too long.
    "You don't have to rush home and cook
        dinner for a hungry
    meat-and-potatoes husband! You can
        have corn flakes if you want!"

Laughing, she waved, and we both slammed
        our doors—
    me off to pick up my kids,
    and her figuring out what she was going
        to scrounge up to satisfy Sam.
Maybe there are some parts to this single
        thing that aren't so bad after all.

One night I lay propped up with every one
        of the six pillows in my bed,
    sipping ice water and reading a really
        good book.
"Just one more chapter," I told myself over
        and over,
    until it was two o'clock in the morning.
I snapped off the light,
    rolled over, and laughed,
    "What husband would put up with me!"
Another hidden plus.

I was invited to a formal dinner dance and
      had nothing suitable to wear.
I spent a whole Saturday scouring the mall
      for bargains.
    I needed something classy, and it didn't
      come cheap.
    A dress that *looked* expensive but wasn't.
I finally settled on a gorgeous black one
    that made me feel like I'd always
      dreamed of feeling.
I realized that any shoes I had would ruin
      the effect, so next came shoes
   and, of course, an evening handbag.
Then I added up what I'd spent that afternoon.
Whoa!
But that was okay by me.
I didn't have to explain that expense to
      anyone.
Another advantage of going it alone.

It's not all bad.
There's freedom.
There's space.
There are people I have been able to spend
      time with.
Places I've been invited to.
Experiences I would have missed.

It's not all bad.
Really.

I'VE SPONGE-PAINTED MY LIFE

Somewhere, I got the crazy idea to sponge-
            paint the boys' bathroom.
I didn't know anything about it.
I just knew I wanted to, so I bought a
            natural sponge and some paint.
When the boys went away for Thanksgiving,
            I decided to plunge in.
Of course, it was 11:30 at night when I
            began.
I have this knack for starting things late at
            night, when I have an energy boost.

Most people would have experimented first
            on paper.
Not me.
Never occurred to me.
I just started in on the wall, up over the tub.
It was pouring outside, and as the rain
            pounded on the roof right above me,
        I sang and laughed and painted, well,
            up a storm.
What I found was this:
        You can make mistakes sponge-
            painting.
        It can look positively messed up.
        But then you can fix it by making more
            sponge marks around it.

136

It's free form, so you can't blow it.
Well, you *can* and I *did* once or twice
    by putting way too much paint on the
        sponge;
    but if you're patient and let it dry,
    it turns lighter, and it's not bad.

I realized I've sponge-painted a lot of my life.
Just plunged in and went for it.
Messed up.
Bad.
But God puts the other sponge marks
        around it
    to blend the mistake.
Time helps dry the dark spots.

When the weekend was over, the boys raced
        up the stairs
    when I told them I had a surprise.
Their reaction was the one word that can
        best be applied to God
    and what He does with our lives:

    AWESOME!

AT ANY COST

I'm not even sure *what* I feel anymore.
   I'm numb.
   I'm weary.
I feel I will never be able to love again.
   Maybe.
   Maybe not.
   Or maybe not in the same way.
Perhaps I've seen—finally—through faintly
      filtering light
   that no one can "fix" my fiercest
   insecurities,
   that no one can be everything to me or
   for me,
   that no one should have the sheer raw
   power that he had over me.
I have the exclusive rights to my own
      completion.
Even with God's guidance, I still have free will.
I can choose.
I want to address my own insecurities and
      fears,
   my own conflicts and inconsistencies.
I want to take responsibility
   for me.

I don't need blame.
I don't need bitterness.
I don't need "how could this happen?"

or even *why?*

I am going on.
I have gone on.
I will make it.

I won't give up because one man wasn't
        strong enough to face the crucial
        issues
    of his life.
His life—not *mine*.
These are not my problems, not my
        responsibility.
I have passed through the muck of
        unresolved issues,
    and although the stickiness clings to my
    shoulders,
    slides down my back,
    and fastens my feet momentarily to the
    floor,
I *am* through it.
I am out.

Out where sunshine permeates my vision
        and helps me see
    what I was unwilling or unable to see
        before.

I wanted love.
I wanted him.
I wanted it to work at any cost.
Haven't I already paid that price before?
Not with as much passion or as much

139

acceptance—or as much fun—
  but I did my time once before and paid
    dearly.
At any cost is too expensive.
It's beyond my budget.

It's me, giving and giving and giving
and then only receiving when it's convenient
    or reluctantly out of guilt.

At any cost won't do anymore.
I've come too far.
And I am no longer a solitary entity:
  I have three big responsibilities,
    three lives that depend on me,
    count on me,
      trust that I'll do what I say.

At any cost wipes out trust.
It ravages lives even as the bright blaze of
    passion sizzles and flares,
      coaxes and dares.

At the very height of wow,
  it still is not worth it
  when you know you'll inevitably step into
  the open doors of the elevator
  and plunge heavily down the shaft.
At any cost would have taken down four this
    time.
I was, so help me God,
  willing to risk it.
How very fortunate for me
  that He was not.

LAURA BETH

"Hey, Mom, I decided to help you," said a
small voice.
I looked down, and there stood Sean next
to me at the sign-out table
for the After School Program.

I had run in quickly to get Neil, after taking
Sean to the orthodontist and
stopping to get balloons for the boy in
my class who had broken his elbow.
I was in such a hurry, I had said,
"Sean, let me run in quick and get Neil!
You wait here!"
and had left him in the car with the
engine running
—something I had never done before or
since—
two feet away from the side door of the
school in which I taught.

"Sean, honey, what are you doing here?" I
asked. "I thought I told you to wait
in the car. Neil and I will be right out."
"Oh, don't worry, Mom," Sean answered
lightly, "I locked the car doors
like you always do!"
"Do you have the keys?" My voice was
beginning to get an edge to it.

"No, I couldn't, they were in the . . . uh-oh!"
　　　　　Sean's voice fell off at the same rate
　　　mine picked up volume.
"Oh, Sean! You *couldn't* have!"
　　　　　(Which, of course, means I couldn't
　　　　　　　have been so stupid
　　　　　as to leave my car running with my
　　　　　　　child in it!)

Yep, he could have, and he did! We all
　　　　　　　raced out,
　　　　　and there was my car running full blast,
　　　　　　　keys locked in,
　　　　　two feet from the side entrance to *my*
　　　　　　　school,
　　　　　in full view of everyone coming to pick
　　　　　　　up their child from After School.
By this time Neil had wandered out
　　　　　and was standing there saying,
　　　　　"What the heck?"
I was trying to hustle them both back into
　　　　　　　the building with some trace of
　　　　　　　dignity,
　　　　　while my temper flared and my heart
　　　　　　　pounded.
One of the parents of a child I had taught
　　　　　　　asked if he could help
　　　　　and went to get a coat hanger to see if
　　　　　　　he could pop the lock up.
　　　　　He tried and tried, but it was no use.
My purse was locked in the car with my
　　　　　　　AAA card,

so I had to look up their number.
No one could find a phone book,
since the school office was already
    locked up.
You can't dial information from the
    school's phone.
I about lost it, right there in my place of
    employment,
    but I took a deep breath and tried to think.
I remembered seeing my spare set of car keys
    on my bedroom dresser.
How could I get them?
"Think, think, think, Lisa," I told myself.
And suddenly, I thought of Laura Beth.

It wouldn't be the first time she had pulled
    us out of a jam.
Wonderful Laura Beth, a college girl we had
    met through the After School
    Program.
We called her our angel and looked forward
    all year to
    the week she took care of the boys
    during Teacher Work Days.
She came up to school to get Jeff when he
    was sick and needed to go home.
She took Neil to his championship soccer
    game and watched him win
    when I had to be at an evening teachers'
    meeting.
Laura Beth knew where I was and when and
    how to get in touch with me.

143

She was onto all my ex-husband's tricks
          with picking up the boys for visits.
She knew how to calm Neil down, how to
          comfort Jeff, and how to
          manage Sean.
And *she* had keys to our house!
Now, if she was only home . . .

I dialed that number and was delighted to
          hear her answer the phone.
No one but Laura Beth would have
          understood my wacky request:
     Could she *please* go to my house,
     unlock the door with her key,
     go up to my bedroom,
     get my extra set of car keys off my dresser,
     bring them up to my school
     (luckily this was all within a mile of
          each other)
     so that I could unlock my car,
     turn off the engine,
     sit down before I collapsed,
     so I could rush off to pick up Jeff at
          day care
     and then deliver the balloons?
She was there in a flash, smiling as always,
     tolerant of my wild ways.

Once again, I would go to sleep with a
          prayer of thanks on my lips
     for Laura Beth,
          for the influence she'd had on all of us,

for her love,
>her time,
>her concern.
She practically helped me raise the boys for
>a good three years or so,
>and for that I will be infinitely thankful.

SOLO SANTA

Well, Christmas tree,
here we are again,
            you and me.
Alone again on Christmas Eve.
You waited here as we went to church.
Then you joyously twinkled your way
      through hot chocolate,
      putting out Santa's cookies,
      hanging the stockings,
      reading,
      toothbrushing,
      goodnight kisses,
      and drinks of water ("Not bathroom
      water, Mom, please! Frigerator water!").
Now they're asleep (I've checked twice!);
      and I can begin the trek from the
      garage,
      where I've stashed their gifts in the
      closet and in my car trunk,
      to the living room.
Here you'll watch
      as I assemble,
      stuff stockings,
      crumble Santa's cookies to make perfect
      crumbs,
      drink eggnog,
      write a note back with my left hand,

146

and check four times to make sure
    everything's out and displayed perfectly.
Then, I'll snap off the lights
    and stumble to my bed at 1:00 A.M.,
        bleary-eyed and weary,
        excited but a little sad.
Surely, there is no night that makes a
        single mom
    feel more alone than Christmas Eve!
Even Mother's Day, without anyone to prompt
        and prod them to do nice things,
or my birthday, which is usually forgotten
        by them
    and celebrated by well-meaning,
    thoughtful friends,
don't cause the utter aloneness of
    solo Santa-ing.

It's hard to not believe
    that your dreams of sharing these
    children in a loving family
    have been stuffed in the stockings along
    with the oranges.
Somehow, tree,
    although your lights flicker on and off
    and Evie's crooning, "Come on, Ring
    Those Bells"—
oh, somehow, brilliant tree,
    I feel as small and crumbled as
        those cookie pieces on the plate for
        Santa.

Universal Miracles

"I can't believe we're here!" whooped Sean.
"Universal Studios here we come!" added
      Jeff.
"All right!" yelled Neil.
We stood at the huge golden globe entrance
      to Universal Studios,
    and I had the weirdest feeling that this
    couldn't possibly
    be happening to us.
Cool vacations were something *other* people
      took
    that we just heard about
    and tried not to be jealous over.
Yet here we stood, and it was indeed Your
      miracle, Lord.

My staff development course on Children's
      Literature had been approved,
    and I received an extra paycheck for
    teaching it.
I had found a wonderful bargain on the
      park passes and on a
    fabulous hotel that had the boys saying,
    "Ooh, we've hit the big times."
I had figured and refigured just how much
      money
    we could afford per person per meal,

and we were even ahead of what I had
    allowed.
Our car had spun out on the cloverleaf exit
    ramp in the pouring rain,
    and even though we did a 360, we
        stayed on the road,
    no one was hurt, and the truck behind
        us stopped
with plenty of room to spare.
In fact, Neil had laughed and said, "Wow,
    Mom! Could you do that *again*?"
And I was actually able to function enough
    to get us to our hotel,
before I shakily fell on my knees in the
    hotel room to thank You, Lord.

More miracles happened as the day went on.
All three boys were unbelievably patient
    waiting in hour-long lines for the rides.
Jeff ended up liking the King Kong ride
    after he had spent the entire time in line
    screaming about not wanting to go on it;
    and I didn't know what to do
    because that was the main ride Sean
    and Neil wanted to go on,
    and I couldn't leave any of them alone.
I know it was Your peace I felt, Lord,
    when I just knew the ride would be
        okay for Jeff
    and was able to ignore the stares of
        people
    who looked like they thought I was an

awful mother
for "making" him go on.
(Where were they when he squealed,
"Whoa, let's do that *again*!
That was *great*!"
as we got off the ride?)
We agreed on most choices, which is a *real*
miracle,
and they all thought it was worth it to
spend
two hours in line for "Back to the
Future,"
which I still can't believe any of them
did!
We found Sean,
who would have been my last guess for
who'd end up lost,
after "only" forty-five minutes (of blood,
sweat, and tears)
instead of the entire rest of the day.
They were excellent sports when the Hard
Rock Café burgers they had so
wanted ended up being out of our
budget.
And when they ended up with only
a Jurassic Park egg filled with candy as
their souvenir,
because that's all we could buy with
what we had left.

We left Universal Studios as four of the last
people out of its gates that night,

with thirty-seven cents left in our
　　backpack,
having been four of the first people in
　　the gates that morning.
We squeezed every drop of its novelty, its
　　excitement, its thrills, its memories.
I believe we appreciated it more than people
　　for whom such things
are commonplace.

So, thank You, Lord, that some of Your
　　miracles,
　　however small they may seem to others,
　　are gigantic wonders in the hearts
　　of the people who need them most.

My Lookouts

My kids have gotten so good,
   they can spot them three booths away.

Is it the lady's smile that seems stuck
   on "trying too hard"?
Or is it the impish-acting children?
Perhaps it's the stiff formality of the man.

Whatever it is, my three guys take one good
      look and pronounce:

> "Single mom
> out to dinner with a date
> and her kids.
> We're guessing first or
> second date . . ."

Sometimes they roll their eyes
   and recount episodes
         that cause me to cringe.

Surely the guys I've gone out with haven't
         been as bad
   as the boys' recollections of them!
What's ironic is to hear them talk about the
         ones they really liked:
      I usually couldn't stand them.

This is a whole new thing; this combination
   of courting and coddling.

Where does one role start and another end?
Is it possible
    to keep them separate but equal?

Maybe it's inconvenient,
                costly,
                and somehow doesn't send the
                right message
                    to either my date or my
                    children
                    to never let the "twain meet."

What's the answer?

What's the question?

TOOTH FAIRY BLUES

The pudgy little hand shook me awake
>before the alarm got me.
"Mommy, he forgot *again*!" a tiny voice piped.
"Huh? What . . . ?" I managed to get past
>my sleep-swollen lips.
"Mommy! *Mommy*!" the voice said again,
>quickly picking up volume
>and persistence.
I sat up and pushed the hair out of my eyes.
Reaching for the clock, I brought it to my
>nose tip:
>5:45 it said.
>Four hours of sleep sure goes fast these
>days.
"Mommy, you *said* try it again. But he still
>forgot!"
"Whaaa? Who?"
I opened my eyes all the way and saw Jeff's
>chin set stubbornly on my high bed.
His eyebrows were furrowed, and his eyes
>held such sadness.
"Oh!" I jumped a good foot off the bed and
>landed next to him. "*Oh, no . . .*"
My heart fell as I remembered that for the
>third night in a row
>I had forgotten to put the Tooth Fairy
>money

under Jeff's pillow.

Quick, I told myself, think fast. "Are you
  sure, honey?"

"Mommy, I looked three times. It's not
  there!"

Well, that shot my distract-him-and-then-
  plant-it-under-the-edge-of-the-
  pillow ploy,
    used so well first on Sean and then on
    Neil.

"How about under the bed?"

"Nope. Looked there too."

Darn! There shot ploy number two. Could I
  possibly push Jeff to a fourth night?
    Or would that make him forever lose
    faith in the Tooth Fairy?

"Hey, what's going on in here?" a sleepy
  Sean croaked, bumbling in.

"Sean, the tooth fairy forgot *again*!"

Did he have to keep saying that? Stab me in
  the heart!

I mean, I felt bad enough. What could I say?
  It had been a busy week. Too many
  practices to take boys to.
    Too many papers to grade. Too many
    plans to make.
    Syllabus due this week for the summer
    course I'm teaching.

"Yeah, that used to happen to me a lot,"
  Sean said.

"It did?"

Unwittingly, Sean had gotten me off the hook.
"Yeah, give him another try. Sometimes he
    takes a night off."
Both Jeff and I looked incredulously at Sean.
With a completely straight face, he nodded
    emphatically.
Joyously, Jeff scampered off to his bedroom,
so quickly that he didn't even notice
    the wink Sean gave
        his eternally grateful mom.

ANOTHER JOB

W_{hat}?
You have another job for me, Lord?
Hey, wait! I already teach first grade all day,
    work at the After School Program,
    tutor children,
    and teach staff development classes—
before I go home to be a mom and tutor to
        my three sons,
    not to mention being a full-time laundress,
    part-time (very part-time) maid,
    and some-time cook. ("Cereal again
        tonight, boys?")

What other job, Lord?
Oh . . . really?
I kind of like the sound of that one.
Okay, I'll try.
But I'll need Your help—big time!
I'll start my new job tomorrow, Lord,
No, today—*right now*.

A most important job, with infinite rewards.
The job of relearning to love myself, of
        accepting myself as I am:
    unflat stomach,
    broken veins,
    and all.
Loving myself as my neighbor.

Lisa Hussey

Doing nice things for myself,
    considerate things,
      yes, even charming things!

And you know what, Lord?
I believe You when You tell me that
this job will make all my other ones easier.

THE OLDEST

Such somber, dark eyes, Lord.
How did they get in my oldest child?
Did I put them there?
I've tried so hard to not add any extra
        pressure.
The oldest doesn't have to be the missing
        parent.
He deserves a childhood too.

But somehow, Lord, even though I didn't
        plan it,
Sean took on more than I'd bargained for.
Was it more than You expected too, Lord?
How do we get the child back and chase
        away this pseudo adult?
How do we get eight-year-old behavior?
The innocence and carefreeness so evident
        in the younger siblings
    is sadly missing in the oldest.
It's not fair.
None of it.

WHITE WATER TRANSFORMATION

Each summer morning
  we donned our bathing suits, T-shirts,
  and water socks,
  grabbed yesterday's towels tumbling in
  the dryer,
  slapped on sunscreen and fanny packs,
  fortified ourselves with dollars, water
  bottles, and season passes,
then piled in our car—
  four doors slamming
    in eager anticipation of White Water!
Our car could find its own way there
  if you just pointed its nose in the right
  direction.

We went timidly that first summer;
  a mom filled with trepidation
  at managing two-, four-, and six-year-
  old boys at the same time.
But for the two hundred dollars down I
    managed to scrape together,
  we had a respite, escape, entertainment,
  and dream vacation all in one.
It was our summer, and dad-gum, it was
    going to work,
  even if we had some kinks to work out
    on the way!

160

Our first kink was the stealing issue.
Would someone steal towels and shoes left
    on a chair?
    Lockers were expensive and a hassle to
        return to—
        what if you were clear on one side
        of the park, tired and hungry,
            and your money was on the
            other side?
        It was a big place, all spread out,
            and little legs move slower as
            the day goes on.
We solved that one quickly:
I wore a fanny pack with the essentials—
        season passes, car keys, money,
    all the irreplaceable stuff—and it went
        wherever I did.
The rest we left on a chair in the middle of
        a lot of chairs and people,
    never isolated and sticking out.

Next was the footwear issue.
The pavement was searing Atlanta-hot both
        in the parking lot
    and waiting for the water rides.
Sneakers were hard to get back on tired,
        swollen feet
    to trudge to the car.
And flip-flops came off on the faster slides.
So we solved this problem with water socks!
Four pairs, even gaudy, hot pink size nines
        for me!

We put them on at home and didn't take
      them off till we got back.
I felt better that our feet were covered
      during the 1,673 trips to the
      bathroom,
         each time wondering *why* I had so
         strongly emphasized
            the no-going-in-the-water rule!

Next was the Mom-can't-see dilemma.
I'm blind without my contacts,
      but I was squeamish about losing one,
      and the bright sun kills my light-
      sensitive eyes with my glasses on.
So I solved that with prescription sunglasses.
      A major purchase but of major safety
      importance—
         you can't keep track of three quick boys
         if you can't see 'em!
Another thing to stash in my fanny pack
      during the rides.

For five summers
      we perfected the White Water routine.
We knew which days to avoid:
      Saturdays and holidays.
The most peaceful times:
      Sunday late-afternoons and evenings,
      any weeknight as the sun was setting.
How to find lost brothers:
      tell any official person with a walkie-
      talkie,

ignore the other two who are saying
maybe somebody stole him,
and *pray*!
What the best food values were:
definitely *not* the ice cream of the future.

And how to gradually, lovingly, and, with
lots of faith,
allow Sean and Neil to go ride one slide
and come back
to Little Squirt's Island where I was
with Jeff.
Then allow two rides.
Then let them go for half an hour.
I watched as Sean forged ahead,
always in the lead,
but Neil was only a half step behind,
being just twenty-two months
younger and very determined.
I saw them look out for one another,
encourage and praise each other
for such daring feats as conquering
scary, in-the-dark Black River Falls
and, finally, that last year, the ultimate:
Dragon Tail Falls.

We grew at White Water!
If anyone watching the calm, confident,
smiling mother
with her well-oiled, three-boy entourage
that last year
had seen the flighty, flustered, befuddled mom

with her darting, dizzying trio of chaos
    of our first year,
she may not have believed us to be the same
    family!

And, in truth, we weren't.

We had grown comfortable with our four-ness.
We no longer thought it was odd to be a
        mom and three boys.
To us, that was normal
        and right
        and good.

We even got to where we stayed after the
        park closed
    for Dive In Movies in the wave pool
and wandered out, hand-in-hand, at midnight
    with the other families
    to the parking lot, sun-weary and
        water-shriveled.

We were White Water regulars.
We had succeeded
    in adapting to the newness of our life.
And we had found the quiet streams of
        The Little Hooch
    on which to float past the harsh realities.

Not Worth It

I have decided
    that I was a fool not to have gone
    through the courts
    for the boys' child support.

Man, if I'd only known *then* what I know *now*!

The expression "squeezing blood out of a
        turnip"
    doesn't even begin to describe it.
I've lost track of the returned/insufficient
        funds checks,
    stopped counting the excuses for lateness.
Why, if the U.S. Postal Service were as bad
        as he says it is,
    none of us would ever get a *thing*.

I have finally faced facts.
He'll only send it when he's forced to send it.
And then
    there's a cost.
To me, but especially to the boys.
Comments to them about my money
        management.
Questions about what it's being spent for.
Phone calls that mess with their minds.
Feelings of entitlement, ownership.
Presumptions.

Asking for what is legally theirs
    stirs up too much,
withdraws too much
    from our emotional bank account,
carries too high a cost.

I'd rather *not* get it
    and do without
than have to put up with the junk
    that accompanies the probably
    worthless checks.

Generous Heart

We share the same birthday,
> interests,
> temperament.

So much alike, it's like loving myself.
It flows, almost effortlessly.

He's there for us.
Generously sharing his large, warm family.
He involves us in a painting party
> before he moves into his new house.

The boys weave in and out of doorways,
> chasing other children through
> empty rooms,
> playing hide-and-seek.

Chinese food,
buffalo wings,
iced drinks
> are interlaced with laughter
> > and music
> > > and the cozy glow of
> > > friendship.

So many times he's made me laugh through
> my tears.

He's given and added and enriched.
But nothing touched me quite as deeply
as the year he gave me so many things for

"our" birthday,
   took the boys and me out to dinner,
      and responded to my, "But I don't
      have anything for you . . ."
         with a smile that will forever
         lodge in my heart.

Knowing I was broke and having car trouble,
   he answered, "I'd like new brakes for
   your car."

Six Boys at Once

"Six boys? Lisa, you are crazy!" my fellow
        teacher and friend said to me
    as we stood in the hall Friday morning.
    "You are really allowing each of your boys
    to have someone spend the night—
    all on the same night—
    after a whole wild week of teaching
    first graders?"
"Yep!" I said. "And I don't think it's such a
        bad idea.
    Every time one of them has someone
    spend the night,
    we end up ordering pizza and
    getting a movie.
    Then I have to hear how
    the other two are bored,
    and when can *they* have someone
    spend the night?
    So I thought, why not kill three stones
    with one pizza?"
"I hadn't thought of it that way,"
        my friend said,
    a new look of puzzled semirespect
    replacing the horrified expression that
    had been on her face.
"Well. At least I hope that's what I'll think at
    ten tonight.

Check with me on Monday morning,
and I'll let you know!"

As it turned out, it was one of the best
        Friday nights in a long time.
Each boy was content, filled to the brim
        with a friend's laughter and
        attention.
I got to read, relax, and spend some much-
        needed quiet time alone.
When the pizza got there, I grabbed my one
        piece before the vultures got it
    and settled with my Diet Coke
    and my blissful silence.
I went down to check every so often, and
        everything flowed along smoothly.
Each pair went to bed, amidst giggles,
        entertaining each other
    with their versions of scary stories.
I went to sleep replete and relaxed,
    waking up early enough to make a
    whole mess of pancakes,
        as the boys put it, for my hungry
        crowd,
        who soon rushed off in their
        different directions
        for various soccer games.

I had done it!
An idea I would have been too fearful and
        nervous to try in the past
    had worked well—no, great!—

because I trusted my instinct that said
I could handle this.
Not only had I handled it,
it had actually done some great things
for my sons.
By making plans early in the week,
it gave them something to look forward to,
something we all need.
It fostered pride in our home, in being
thankful for what we *did* have,
instead of what we didn't.
It showed the boys' friends what a loving,
creative family we had.
It helped my boys build solid friendships,
and it also resulted in their being asked
to other people's homes.
It gave me a chance to get to know their
friends.
And sometimes, when a friend's attitude or
actions were less than desirable,
it showed me what a good job I really
was doing
(although I doubted it quite often).

Thank You, Lord, for the courage to step
out and try new things,
things that benefit my sons and myself,
things that make us stronger and surer,
more resilient, more secure.

Thank You that *new* is no longer frightening
and overwhelming.

That what has replaced fear is confidence in
who You are
and in what You promise to always be.

Thank You for the confidence to handle
six boys,
all on the same night!

WHAT I CANNOT BE

I can be a lot of things, Lord,
like tear wiper, dream repairer, hope
restorer.
I'm a heck of a mom sometimes; just okay
most of the time.
And yes, I have my horrendous moments too.
I'm a cook, laundress, tutor,
storyteller, historian, chauffeur,
housekeeper, social secretary,
cheerleader,
nurse, doctor, counselor,
mender of feelings,
builder of values.

But there's one thing I cannot be:

a father.

There is a tightness that binds my heart
when the notices come home
for the father/son picnics and the
Pinewood Derbies.

I cannot breathe.

My family's so far away that uncles and
grandfather are not an option.
Who will be my sons' step-in father? Who
has the time, the desire?

Sean's baseball coach rose to the occasion:
    he took time off work to attend the
    kindergarten father/son picnic.
A large man sitting humbly cross-legged on
        my college bedspread,
    eating the lunch I had sent along for the
    two of them.
Happy to be there.
No, "Thrilled!" his wife later told me.
A good man, a blessing who ended up
        being blessed
    by a proud little guy who kept
    introducing him as *my* coach.

Three years later
    it would be the husband of a dear friend
who stepped forward
    to handle the awesome task of designing
    and constructing
        the Pinewood Derby car that would
        come in third place
            in the whole competition!

What I cannot be,
    God will provide.

I just have to have a little faith
    and lots of friends—
or is it lots of faith
    and a few very carefully selected
    friends?

HEAD HELD HIGH

I remember the night, Lord.
It's emblazoned on my mind forever.

I pull up the picture, the feeling,
    when Sean has just kicked Neil
    and Neil has called him a moron
    and Jeff is whining about no fair.

It was a sultry July night in Sarasota.
We had been at the beach all day, just the
        four of us,
    on a vacation that we had all planned
    and that I had paid for with money I'd
    earned
        teaching an extra class.
We were salty, a bit burned, and ravenous.
We felt that sun-drain kind of tired:
        weary but content,
        wanting to be served,
        not wishing to do anything
                that required effort.

We found an ad for a restaurant in a tourist
        guide.
I called and got directions; we donned our
        spiffiest shorts; and we all
    jumped in the car.
When we arrived, the place was fancier than

175

I'd thought,
    and I was dismayed.
It was late, and we'd already gotten lost
        three times on the way.
And now we were past hungry!
The maître d', seeming to sense my
        hesitance,
    beamed a hearty, "Right this way!"
    and seated us like royalty by the
        window.
The view was gorgeous—lights twinkling
        across the inlet water.
The food superb—crab-stuffed shrimp
        melting on my tongue.
We had two waiters who gently teased the
        boys
    and smiled warm strength to me.

I do not remember their names,
but I shall never forget their words to me,
        "You have a lovely family, ma'am.
        I know you must be
            so very proud of them."
        "What nice manners these boys
            have!"
        "You can sure tell these guys are
            crazy about their mother!"

Oh, that was honey to my heart,
        steel for my soul,
        kindling for the flame of my spirit!

I wonder if those two kind young men

knew the magnitude of the gift they
    gave me
on that balmy, sweet July evening.

For those beautiful moments,
    perched among white starched linen
    and crystal glasses,
        I breathed success.

I had done it! The impossible!
I was flat raising three boys alone!
And doing one heck of a job of it.

I *glided* out of that restaurant,
    head held high,
    back straight.

I was one incredible lady that night.

And, oh, Lord, I have never forgotten it!

LIKE BUTTERFLIES

I've learned to hold them, Lord, openhanded,
    like butterflies.
These flighty, flitting, fearless sons of mine.
They're borrowed, from You, Lord, really.
Mine only in the sense of heredity and
        responsibility.

I am to train them up in the way they
        should go,
not clutch them in my fists,
    smothering their spirits,
    crushing their filmy, brilliant wings
        with my fear and worry.

They perch on my outstretched hand,
    which is palm up,
    facing You.

Sean:
    so fast, so light.
    At times shy, then brash,
    trying to make his way in the world,
    stamping his mark on all he touches
        to make it truly his.

Neil:
    impulsive, daring, aggressive.
    Defensive yet sensitive,
    generous yet defiant.

The tester of limits and of authority.

Jeff:
>slow-moving, heavy on his feet,
>solid and methodical.
>Impish grin, loud voice,
>resisting growing up, pulling back, fearful,
>a lover of books, of knowledge,
>>of people.

These are the three sons You've given me—
who giggle together
>as easily as they punch each other in the
>stomach or face,
who call each other stupid
>and make light of each others' short-
>comings and mistakes.
But who also amazingly come through for
>>each other
>at the most unpredictable times.
Who are twisted together as tightly
>as three strands in a rope.

It's so tempting, Lord,
>to grab them protectively to my chest,
>to keep them from hurtful words,
>to shelter them from injuries and injustice.
But I can't, can I, Lord?

Only You can do that.
Only You can keep them in Your
>tender care.

I am to feed them vegetables,
                vitamins,
                and Your Word;
clothe them, take their temperatures;
teach them money responsibility,
                manners,
                morals;
wipe their tears;
listen to them;
learn from them;
love them.
      Oh, yes, Lord, *love* them!

You have given me such a privilege, Lord:
to raise three boys
      into men of God,
      men of integrity.

Butterflies with wings of steel,
      who can always light
      on my outstretched, uplifted hands.